BO

An enjoyable path, this book is a must read for anyone venturing outside of their comfort zone or reaching outside of their old paradigms. We are all entertainers on some level, and Barbara has shared all the best of her experiences in both the entertainment and business worlds to help guide us down an easy- to-follow path to our own full potential. She has put them together in a very eloquent, yet fun and easy-to-read manner. What a gift she offers us—a *logical* life guide whether our stage is in a theatre or in the corporate world. Going from the New York stage myself to Screen Actors Guild member to business owner and operator to running multiple automotive franchises, I know firsthand that the "Turino Method" works! My successes were enhanced because of my stage training and acting abilities. What has spoken to me from Barbara's work is that this method not only guides one's transition into business but can be applied to all stages of one's personal life. What is your stage? Encore! Encore!

Paula Caravella
Automotive General Manager
CEO/DVS Fence Company, Inc
Sr. Relationship Manager/
Capital One Auto Finance

As a wedding photographer, I need to "perform" for my clients on one of the most important days of their lives. Having spent many years working in community theater, I am able to use the skills I learned onstage to make my clients feel at ease, or give them a small taste of the theatrical themselves——letting them take center stage for their big day. Even if you've never performed onstage before, Barbara's book details how you, too, can use the magic of the theater to enhance your interactions with your clients and take your business to a whole new level of performance.

Scott Fischbein
Ready For Your Close Up
Photographer, Davis, CA

If you want an Oscar-winning performance in life or in your career, then this is the book for you! Barbara Turino is no act. She's the real deal, with tons of tips and techniques that can put you on the red carpet to success and fulfillment.

John Putzier
Senior Professional in Human Resources
Author of *Get Weird* and
Weirdos in the Workplace

Getting Your Act Together is a must-read book for those who want to embrace and experience life with a sense of passion, purpose, and productivity in their personal as well as their professional lives.

Tom McQueen, PhD
President, American Family Foundation, Inc.
Author of *Letters to Ethan*

Barbara's book is intelligent and inspirational. A must-read for actors transitioning into the business world. The notion that the role is YOU and your stage is anywhere and everywhere will make perfect sense to any actor and will help take the fear out of redirecting their career.

Ivan Rutherford
Actor (performed the role of
"Jean Valjean" in *Les Miserables*
on Broadway, national tours,
and regional theatres)

A good teacher must be animated, illuminating, and entertaining. A successful politician or lawyer must be captivating and charismatic. Now with the creative and artful guidance of Barbara Turino's *Getting Your Act Together,* anyone can be motivating, achieving, and productive by putting the actor's performance techniques into one's professional and personal life. A truly eye-opening account of how to put the "show" into business.

Ellen Wagner, MA
Educational Therapist RST, LH
Owner of The A Team & Study Buddies

Having enjoyed and performed in theater since I can remember, I definitely can attest some of the learned theater skills to my current knowledge of business today. For me, I would attribute the ability to speak and perform in front of others without getting nervous as invaluable. Barbara Turino knows how to take these learned theater skills and apply them in business. She has helped my company, Crescent Solutions, understand many of our shortcomings and showed us ways in which to improve them. I recommend her and this book to anyone looking to improve their personal or business acumen!

Brian Fischbein
Chief Executive Officer, Crescent Solutions
Member YPO and Gennext
Founder of The Society and Captiv8

Getting Your Act Together

HOW TO PUT THE SHOW INTO BUSINESS

BARBARA TURINO

Myladian Press
Tustin, CA 92782

www.gettingyouracttogether.com

ISBN: 978-0-578-09110-5

Printed in the United States of America

Author's Photo: Scott Fischbein

Cover Design and Original Page Illustrations: Lollie Ortiz

Editorial Assistance: Betsy Bloudin

Contents

*This book is dedicated to my two leading men,
costarring with me on my journey of life.*

*To my sons, Scott and Brian, your never-ending
support, encouragement, and gentle hands on my
back have enabled me to move closer to my potential.
You are my life, my legacy, and the very best of me.
I look forward to watching and supporting you
on your life's journey.*

*A special thank you to my two original producers,
my dad, Phil, who is shining his spotlight on me from
above, and my mom, Rhoda, who continues to light
my way and direct me every day.*

Chapter 1

There's no people like show people, They smile when they are low

Attitude vs. Behavior

("There's No Business Like Show Business"
from *Annie Get Your Gun* —Lyrics by Irving Berlin)

"Thirty minutes to places!" shouts the stage manager. I find a quiet place and think about my character: Who is my character? Where is she coming from right now, and where is she going? What is she feeling? What do I want the audience to know, feel, experience, and learn about my character? What is the message I hope to convey to them by playing my character?

"Fifteen minutes to places!" I take deep breaths and relax. Meditating, I concentrate on my breathing, slow myself down, and think about achieving my goals and about being a great success. I picture the audience applauding for my performance at the end of the show.

"Five minutes to places!" Concentrating, I take a few more deep breaths and let my excitement build and my adrenaline with it.

"PLACES PLEASE!" Any minute, the curtain will rise, and I will be someone else for the show's duration. I am ready!

CURTAIN UP

For the next couple of hours, which pass like only minutes, I perform at the height of my potential. I do everything as I've rehearsed it, and the audience responds. They laugh when I want them to laugh, and they cry when I want them to cry. They hang on my every word.

Before I know it, the show is over. As I walk on stage for my curtain call, the crowd cheers. They rise to their feet and applaud, and as I look around to see who else is on stage, I realize that I am by myself. Their applause is for me alone. What a feeling! I did my best, and I received recognition and appreciation for my achievement and the effort I put into it. There is nothing in the world quite like that feeling.

Having been lucky enough to experience the euphoria that comes with applause for a job well done, I intend to use this book to help you understand—indeed, experience—this incredible feeling. Even if you never get on a theatrical stage, your journey through this book will allow you to see how the emotional highs and lows of performing on stage contrast with your "performances" in your professional life and personal life.

Learning and practicing the techniques that an actor uses to be successful on stage can help motivate you to become a true performer, enjoying the success, the newfound meaning, and, yes, the ovations that can come with that.

Did you ever wonder why actors volunteer to perform in community theaters, rehearsing up to twenty hours a week, for no pay? And why do even the most successful movie and television actors often aspire to perform on Broadway? They don't do it for the money—the money doesn't even compare to the money you can earn in television and the movies.

Take Jerry Lewis, a successful movie and television personality, who throughout his career aspired to do one thing: he wanted to perform on

Broadway. In 1995, he finally got his chance to premiere in a Broadway revival of *Damn Yankees*, leading to a nationwide tour. Lewis, who was wonderful in the role of the Devil, reported a feeling of fulfillment he had never experienced before. It is for this feeling that performers choose their profession. Learning, and then working, to perform at your best and being appreciated for your effort is what makes the sometimes difficult journey of a performer worthwhile.

Performers perform for the applause. They perform for the strong sense of accomplishment that a successful performance brings. And they perform for the personal challenge.

In *On Cue*, an actor's newsletter, editor Dave Myers wrote the following:

> People who aren't involved in theater probably just wouldn't understand. It can be a lot of work and a lot of stress. Each spring, there are a lot of people scratching their heads, trying to figure out just how to make that mammoth set mobile. Maybe they are thinking about whether they can construct a whole new set in time for opening night. Directors are trying to figure out which part of the play that they can pull out and have the show still make sense. Costumers are trying to get back that costume that they borrowed before. A whole group is rehearsing the choreography of moving a complete set for a new scene in just a few moments. And we call this fun. It is fun. Ask anyone involved in theater.

In a speech written more than thirty-five years ago, Jeanette Henn, president of *ACT*, an organization for actors in Cincinnati, Ohio, addresses why the performers, both then and now, are here:

> In today's analytical world we find ourselves called upon to explain our interest in the theater as an avocation, to justify it, even to defend it—explanation and defense needed only for those who do not share in this fascinating, exasperating, warm-hearted, cold-blooded, artistic, and crazy world that is theater.

It is all of that: a contradictory state of mind that defies analysis. So, we wonder why we impulsively follow this interest of community theatre—an interest that consumes our time, taxes our brains, and tries our patience—and do it as a form of relaxation, outside of the hours of our respective occupations. Well, because ... we know only that when the show is put together—after four to six weeks of rehearsals, set construction, efforts of the production crews, publicity committees, ticket sales—when the lights go up on opening night, the show is a good one and the patrons like it. That answers the question—or, rather, it eliminates the question.

Acting is the reality of doing. It is acting real in pretend situations and pretending in real situations.

Christina Ricci, when interviewed, said, "I loved acting; it made me happy because you're able to express everything you can't express in your normal, everyday life."

Throughout this book, I will reveal proven techniques used by thespians, as well as Actor's Critical Tips, that you can apply to both your professional life and your personal life. You will learn how to master a part, how to play a role, how to switch the switch, how not to take rejection personally, how to set goals, how to play the game to win, and how to perfect your performance so that you truly look and feel your part, all at the same time. I sincerely hope that you will be entertained and yet also learn how to give award-winning performances, earn standing ovations, experience the thrill of applause, and merit rave reviews. You'll be getting your act together—putting the show into business, every time.

PLACES EVERYONE!

"All the world's a stage, and all the people merely players," writes Shakespeare, who knew the secret to success long before our day. The entire world is a stage, and we are on it every day. We cannot afford to miss opportunities to get our act together and razzle-dazzle our audience.

Consider the following scenario and how you would react. You go to the theater for an evening's entertainment. You pay your hard-earned money for the tickets and expect to be entertained. But just before the show begins, the director comes on stage to make an announcement: "Thank you for coming to our show tonight. We appreciate your patronage. However, I'd like to take this time to offer you an apology ahead of time. Our lead actor has had a terrible day. His kids are failing in school, his dog is ill, and he's suffering from a terrible headache. We know you'll understand and hope you'll forgive us if his performance is only mediocre tonight. After all, we all have bad days! We thank you for your understanding and for your continued support of our theater."

Ridiculous, right? There's no way we would put up with that kind of behavior. As an audience member or as a consumer, we don't think about what kind of a day an actor or service provider has had; we simply don't want it to interfere with his performance, and thus with our entertainment, or our satisfaction as customers. We consider the performer a professional and expect from him the very best that he has to offer. We will settle for nothing less, and we won't come back if we are disappointed.

Why do we expect any less from ourselves when we go to our jobs? We, too, are professionals, no matter what we do. Our customers, managers, and coworkers expect our best, regardless of whether we're having a bad day or what emotions we're experiencing. Behavior we would never excuse in the theater is tolerated in business every day.

Like actors, we must be conscious of our performance, striving to prevent our own attitude, whatever it is, from adversely affecting our behavior or interaction with our valued customers. Therefore, let's have an attitude adjustment, or—better yet—let's accept for now the premise that our feelings on any given day are unimportant to our customers, bosses, coworkers, and, at times, family members. In a professional performance role, all that is important is your behavior. If you *act as if* you are a professional who is expected to perform at her highest level, then how you feel becomes secondary.

When people act as they are expected, and maybe even required, to behave (good training helps), they provide the superior service and memorable behavior that a customer truly recognizes and appreciates. And if a customer tells others how pleased he was with the service he received, that becomes just another way of receiving a standing ovation. Whether you realize it or not, you are on stage all day, every day, and so must consciously give your very best performance regardless of how you feel.

Obviously always be true to yourself. Relax and have fun with your life. But realize that most of the time, especially in professional situations, your performance needs to be your best. The famous television host Dr. Phil McGraw says on his show, "Behave your way to success." Similarly, Dr. Laura Schlessinger preaches every day on her radio talk show that "[y]our feelings are not important—your actions are."

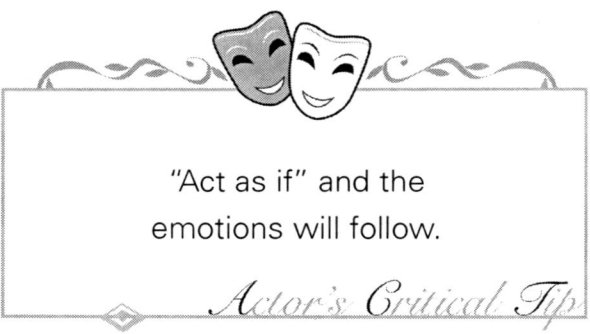

"Act as if" and the
emotions will follow.

Actor's Critical Tip

An interesting phenomenon occurs when you learn this technique and practice it. Because feelings are brought about by actions, you will actually begin to feel the way you are acting. When you *act as if*, the emotions will follow. The law of reversal means that you can act your way into feeling. Most people wait until they feel a certain way and then act on those feelings. Sometimes they act out a feeling that is inappropriate, like when they wake up on the wrong side of the bed, yell at their spouse and children, and then go to work and treat their customers to a poor performance. And in such a mood, that often means that an angry employee mishandles an angry customer. So much for customer service!

Many people believe that their behavior can't be pleasant unless they feel happy. They find it difficult to act in ways that don't reflect their emotional state at a given moment. But the law of practice states that practice develops habits.

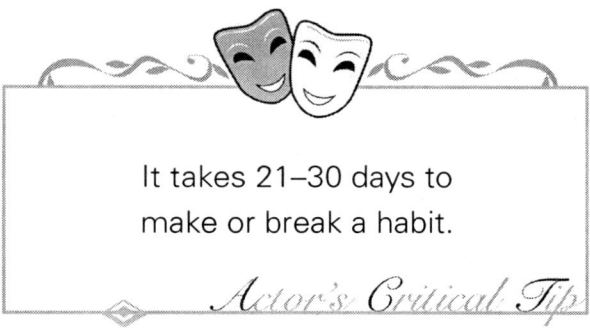

It takes 21–30 days to
make or break a habit.

Actor's Critical Tip

Creating a new habit will not make you feel comfortable or sincere at first. In fact, it will take all of the acting skills you possess. The good news, however, is that if you practice acting in the ways you want to feel, then, almost magically, you will start to feel that way. I once heard a general manager of a very successful automotive dealership tell his employees, "Act enthusiastic and you will be enthusiastic." Another example is Alan Alda. During an interview after the World Trade Center attacks, he commented on being asked to sing in a celebrity tribute of "New York, New York" along with many other stars. Alda wasn't sure whether he would be able to pull it off and keep his composure, so he decided to just "act [his] way back to normalcy." Humphrey Bogart said it best: "The only thing you owe the public is a good performance."

Employees often expect a certain attitude from managers. They want to know how their managers feel about them. Are they liked and respected on a personal level? Managers, on the other hand, often complain about the bad attitudes of some employees.

Here is my out of-the-box solution: IT IS NOT IMPORTANT! Take your attitude and feelings out of the equation. Employees should expect managers to behave in a respectful way regardless of what the manager is thinking or feeling. Employees need to let their managers know that they expect to be treated with respect and courtesy and they will treat their managers the same way. Managers, conversely, can expect certain behaviors from their employees and should make those requirements clear and in writing.

Two wonderful phrases, both of which are helpful to keep in mind for giving feedback or coaching, are "I understand the emotion—but the behavior is inappropriate" and "A good argument does not change the reality of the situation." Every day, each of us makes choices, both consciously and unconsciously, to behave or act in certain ways. Although many believe that feelings cannot be controlled, everyone is responsible for his actions—for the way he acts. We can choose appropriate behavior regardless of our thoughts and feelings, no matter how intense they are within us. That is not to say, however, that we should not be in touch with our feelings. It is helpful to understand what you are feeling at any given moment, and it is not always possible to prevent yourself from feeling a certain way. However, you decide whether you act on your feelings.

To be successful at your work and in your life, you must often act appropriately despite what you feel. When you are having a bad day, when all sorts of things are going wrong, you may feel grumpy or angry. But when you arrive at your job and inter*act* with your customers, managers, and coworkers, you can choose to be professional, friendly, and courteous in spite of your feelings, rather than acting with anger. Although we cannot always choose our feelings about events in our work life or personal life, it is crucial that we consciously choose appropriate responses.

I am in no way suggesting that our behavior should be fake or false. On the contrary, our behavior must be governed by a sincere desire to provide service or the customer will see right through our actions as only a façade. Stay consciously aware of your established goals: to exceed customers' expectations and provide the highest level of customer service possible. Examine your feelings and thoughts and ask yourself, "What behaviors should I exhibit right now that will best reflect my mission and core values?" Ultimately, the quality of your life is directly dependent upon the choices you make.

Actors, of course, understand this concept and know that the show must go on. The audience never knows what the actors are personally thinking and feeling; we have no idea who the actors truly are—and that is by design. The only persona we see is the one they want us to see. (Perhaps that is why so many people like to read the tabloids: they want to get the inside scoop, to find out that some actor is not really as nice as he appears on the screen or the stage.)

The same is true for professionals. Being professional at all times requires that we act like professionals.

In Sanford Meisner's book *Sanford Meisner on Acting*, the famous teacher says, "An ounce of behavior is worth a pound of words." He tells his students to be real on stage—to really *do* it, not just act like they are doing it. "If you are really doing it, you don't have time to watch yourself doing it," Meisner says to his students during an acting exercise. "Nobody gives a damn how you feel, you know? NOBODY CARES! We care when your concern about how you feel hurts your exercise."

Can you guess what kinds of professionals know how to use acting skills proficiently? Did you guess lawyers? You should have. Have you ever seen a more talented group of actors? They could have sold tickets to some of the more infamous trials of our time. Think of O.J. Simpson's trial, for example. Simpson's lawyers pulled out every professional trick in the book to convince the jury that their client was indeed telling the truth. Remember how O.J., a professional actor, behaved while trying on the leather glove to see whether it fit him? Whether or not you believe O.J. was guilty, you have to admit it was quite a performance.

Alice Sebold, in her memoir *Lucky*, writes what her lawyer told her as they prepared to address the grand jury at the end of the trial of the man who raped her, "Well, the grand jury is made up of twenty-five civilians, and we're onstage." She described her lawyer's demeanor: "Gail did as she said she would. She used a courtroom manner. She made a lot of eye contact with the jurors, used hand gestures, and spent time enunciating key words or phrases she wanted them to note and remember." Ms. Sebold writes, "As I left that courtroom I felt I had put on the best show of my life."

Most great teachers have mastered the art of turning the classroom into a stage. To keep their students engaged, teachers use their acting skills to perform, whether they feel like it or not. For lawyers, the courtroom is the stage. For teachers, the classroom is the stage. What is your stage? Is it your office, the customer service counter, the retail store?

The next time your feelings or attitude start to determine your actions or behaviors, remember the story from the beginning of this chapter, get your act together, smile, and *act as if* all is well. You are a professional on stage with a job to do. Remembering this will help you to exceed the expectations of all those with whom you come into contact. The late Marlon Brando said it well: "Everyone has suffered moments when you are thinking one thing or feeling one thing and not showing it. That is acting."

Shirley MacLaine sums it up beautifully in her book *I'm Over All That* when she says, "All life, even the cruelest drama and most absurd comedy, is a form of show business, a kind of performance, and I have been lucky enough to have created the moving picture show of my own life. I have starred in it, produced it, written it, directed it—even financed and distributed it. What's even better is that I get to rerun it now and then, to see things I might have missed back then." Shirley says, "I learned long ago that living *is* acting, and it always has been. Every day we choose what script we will write for ourselves, how we will play our part, what wardrobe we will wear, and what emotions we will allow ourselves to feel or to repress." She goes on to say, "I am the writer, producer, wardrobe mistress, star, and director of my own play every day that I live."

What will be your life's show? Will you be a star and get rave reviews and standing ovations? I hope this book helps you do just that. Start by waking up each day and saying to yourself, "Oh What a Beautiful Morning" (*Oklahoma*)—and remember that "There's No People Like Show People, They Smile When They Are Low" (*Annie Get Your Gun*).

IT'S SHOWTIME!
TIPS AND TOOLS

Right now you may be thinking, *Easier said than done. How do I motivate myself to do that?* I'll share some techniques that have worked for me.

Switch the switch

When I am about to enter into a situation, whether in my professional role or in preparation for stepping into my character role on stage, I visualize a switch just like a light switch behind my neck. In my mind, I reach behind my neck and vividly picture myself flipping the switch on. This helps me to turn off all my own thoughts, feelings, and emotions and to act as if I am excited and ready to perform my part. It works and has served me well many times when I was exhausted or sick or for some other reason did not feel like working, rehearsing, or even performing. This technique has worked for me in every situation I've tried it in. Whether you are feeling fear, anxiety, tension, anger, or fatigue, you can choose any behavior that is appropriate to your situation by flipping the switch, despite your own feelings.

Showtime

Disney World provides many opportunities to experience the magic of acting. The Disney Institute in Orlando conducts a wonderful training program, which includes an underground tour. Underneath the Wonderful World of Disney is a complex series of tunnels from which and into which characters and vendors emerge and disappear unobtrusively. On the back of some of the doors leading to the grounds is one word: "Showtime." Others say "Remember Your Smile."

One company I know adapted this Showtime philosophy. When people ask, "What time is it?" someone always answers, "It's Showtime!" Occasionally, one of the employees gets on the intercom first thing in the morning, just before unlocking the doors to the customers, and announces, "Good morning, people! Do you know what time it is? It's Showtime!" The company has also printed placards saying "Showtime!" that have been placed in all the company offices. Morale at the company is high, and people act as if they love their jobs. I believe they really do.

Similarly, this belief that business is a "show" is evident in everything Disney does. Employees are called "cast members," uniforms are known as "costumes," jobs are "roles in the show," and customers are "guests." Disney makes sure to separate "backstage" from the "onstage"—all company business is kept separate from guest business. What a great philosophy!

Do your customers ever observe employees backstage or overhear conversations that are not meant for customers' ears? Do you protect the magic, vision, and philosophy you are selling every day? Do you have a "Showtime" philosophy?

Go Fish!

I highly recommend the wonderful little book *Fish!* by Stephen C. Lundin, Harry Paul, and John Christensen. *Fish!* is based on the story of the Pike Place Fish Market in Seattle. In the foreword to *Fish!,* Ken Blanchard says that its contents will motivate people to take pride in what they do. One of the characters in the book quotes Sara Ban Breathnach's book *Simple Abundance:* "Most of us are uncomfortable thinking of ourselves as artists. But each of us is an artist. With every choice, every day, you are creating a unique work of art. Something that only you can do. The reason you were born was to leave your own indelible mark on the world."

Do you see yourself as an artist with the opportunity to create each day? *Fish!* explains four concepts that make the Pike Place Fish Market successful not only as a business but as a training process for other businesses:

- Choose Your Attitude
- Find Ways to Play
- Make Your Customer's Day
- Be There

I suggest that you consider using the *Fish!* book and videos to help you create a company where people have fun, engage with customers, and act as if they are in the best show on earth.

Code of conduct

Create a code of conduct for all employees and include a list of behaviors that are expected from both employees and managers. First, develop a mission or vision statement, taking the time to identify your core values. After doing that, create a list of behaviors that support your values and mission. These might include eye contact, firm handshakes, professional greetings, and appropriate dress, to name just a few examples. Use these behaviors to evaluate employees, and hold them accountable for their actions. The following chapter will help you explore how to develop a mission statement that supports your core values.

My Way

FIND YOUR PASSION

Chapter 2

And more, much more than this, I did it my way

Find Your Passion

("My Way" — Written by Paul Anka, Sung by Frank Sinatra)

Actors live to act. They love the whole process, from the audition and the first read-through to the rehearsals, the sets, and the costumes to tech week and, finally, to opening night and the rest of the run. Acting is a passion. When an actor enters the rehearsal hall, real life stays outside the doors. For hours, the actor is transformed into someone else. To learn lines and blocking (where to stand on stage as lines are delivered), actors must give total concentration to the task at hand. If they are tired or upset, they cannot let their feelings intrude; doing so will affect the actor's performance. This takes a great deal of concentration, but feels great. Acting is about stepping out of your life and escaping into the process.

People tell me that playing a sport fulfills a similar need; for me, acting does it. I am reasonably sure I will never be discovered. And you know what? I don't care! I love acting, and I often do it for free. It sounds crazy, I know. Occasionally I have been paid for acting, but when I am, I always feel as if I am taking money under false pretenses. My son, Brian, said it best: At the age of twelve, he was cast by a local dinner theater and paid $100 a week. His comment on receiving his first paycheck was, "Mom,

I don't understand why they are paying me. If they asked me, I would have been willing to do this part for free."

I feel the same way. The roles I have played have been right for me, and I have done a good job with them. Being onstage at least one or two times a year usually fulfills my need. However, if I go a long time without getting a part, withdrawal sets in, and my desire to get a role in a show becomes a strong need. I have found a partial solution in a career I love and a hobby I adore. In the past few years, both have been going well, and I've wondered whether a correlation between the two exists. I thought long and hard, spoke with people I trust and respect, and discovered that, yes, such a correlation does exist. The skills I use to make me successful at my avocation help me to be successful in my business life, and vice versa.

In my professional life, I am a facilitator, trainer, consultant, and executive business coach helping companies to improve their performance and thereby exceed both their expectations and the expectations of their customers and to ultimately increase their sales and thus their profits. This is accomplished through training, process improvement, and, often, employee involvement.

My avocation is acting. After discovering the crossover of skills and talents that existed for me, I began to wonder whether I could use this information to help individuals and companies grow. My personal mission statement has always been *to help people grow and move toward their full potential.* It has served me well in my roles as teacher, spouse, mother, friend, and business consultant.

The opportunity to use my acting skills to help me become a better consultant is exciting. I have two goals when I train or conduct a workshop. First, I want everyone present to learn something. If each person can say that they learned a new skill, a new fact, a new way of doing something, or a new way of looking at something after spending time with me, then I have achieved my first goal. The second, but equally important, goal is that during this learning process we all have fun. By using the same techniques as actors, I can make doing business not only easier but more fun.

Because I have recognized that performing is my PASSION, I have found a career that lets me perform on stage daily in some very obvious ways. Whether you realize it or not, you, too, are on stage every day. As a consultant and a trainer, I get up in front of groups to do presentations, workshops, and training—and sometimes they even applaud at the end! This brings some of the same feelings into my professional life that acting brings into my personal life.

In one episode of the television show *Ally McBeal*, Mariah Carey, starring as herself, traveled around with a spotlight and a techie who lit her up whenever she needed to shine. Sometimes I wish I had someone to do that for me. My personality type is that of socializer. My type of personality likes to be in the spotlight, to be the life of the party. My occupation helps to fulfill my need to be creative, to perform, and to be recognized for a job well done. It is not exactly the same as landing a lead role in a great show, but it comes close. For me there is no business like show business—so I put the show into my business.

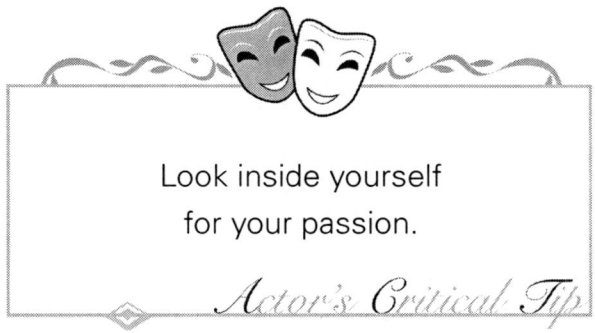

Look inside yourself
for your passion.

Actor's Critical Tip

Ask yourself, "Do I have a passion for something? Can I fulfill that passion in my vocation as well as my avocation?" Some people are lucky to work at a job they love, but many just work a job, period. The answer to the dilemma might be twofold. If you cannot find your passion in your work, then spend lots of time on your passion outside of work. Fill your free time doing what you love to do. Plan for fun! By scheduling free time for your hobbies and joys, you'll have something to look forward to.

Find your bliss and schedule it into your life. Make it a priority because the outside world won't.

If possible, choose your life's work with an eye to including your passion, or finding your passion, in your work. How do you find your passion? One of the best ways to bring passion into your work or even to discover your passion in the first place is to look inside yourself. Examine what is important to you to discern what you really value. Then develop a mission or a vision. As Jacqueline Kennedy Onassis once said, "An aim in life is the only fortune worth finding."

I heard one of the best examples of combining passion and mission when I was privileged to meet Dr. Charles Garfield, a renowned author, speaker, and college professor who was a computer scientist on the Apollo 11 project that sent the first men to the moon. Dr. Garfield was a keynote speaker at a conference I attended where he told the incredible story of the Apollo team of dedicated scientists who had worked for little pay under far less than ideal conditions for hours and hours on end because of a burning passion to succeed.

Dr. Garfield went on to research high-achieving individuals, teams, and organizations to uncover the qualities they share in common. He details his findings in his book *Peak Performers*, and the advice he gives is to choose a career that fuels your passion, makes your heart race and your eyes twinkle, and gets you leaping out of bed each morning. Find passion in your work or create it. If you love people but are in a job that requires paperwork that you hate, consider hiring someone to do the paperwork, leaving you free to do the people work. "To be successful", says Dr. Garfield, "you must have passion and a system. Failure results when you have passion but no system or a system but no passion. The biggest motivating factor, he says, is the desire to be proud of ourselves in pursuit of something we care deeply about."

I will never forget the story Dr. Garfield related at the end of his presentation. He told of his success working on the Apollo mission and his pride watching the men land on the moon. When the landing was televised, Charles watched with his grandfather. As they watched, his grandfather remarked that it was impossible for men to walk on the moon. As hard as Charles tried, he could not convince his grandfather that what he was seeing was really happening. His grandfather insisted that it was television magic. Finally, after Charles explained to his grandfather the details of all the work that he and his team had done to accomplish the mission, his grandfather, stunned, said in no uncertain terms that he was witnessing a miracle. Charles realized then that "one person's job is another person's miracle." He states that "in this era, anybody who doesn't believe in miracles is simply not a realist."

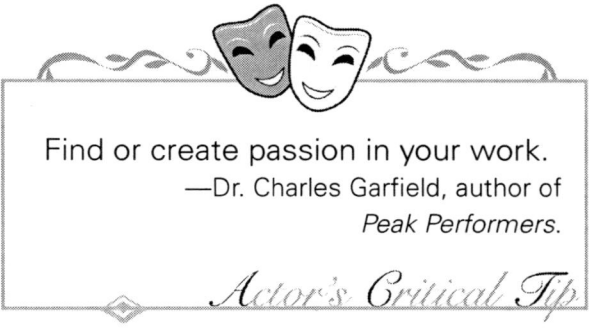

Find or create passion in your work.
—Dr. Charles Garfield, author of
Peak Performers.

Actor's Critical Tip

Once you clearly define your mission, vision, and purpose and understand what bliss means to you, make those joyful things part of your everyday life.

All this became clear to me one day when my older son, Scott, asked his brother, Brian, and me, as we were leaving for yet another rehearsal, "How can you spend so much time and work so hard at something that doesn't pay you anything?" Some months later, Scott was bitten by the theater bug—and it has been a big part of his life ever since. He has not asked that question again.

Scott's question was a good one. Why do people work so hard and spend so much time for little or no pay? Rehearsals can take six to eight weeks or more and sometimes fifteen to twenty hours during each of those weeks. Community theater actors also help build the set and, at the end of the run, strike (disassemble) it, collect props, and make or find appropriate costumes. They also do their own publicity, produce and sell ads for programs, run lights, produce, and direct—and the list goes on and on. Why do they do it?

They do it because actors have a deep passion for their craft. Creating a show and developing a character is an awesome achievement. Setting a goal and creating a great show is pay enough when it earns you recognition for a job well done, and the applause of the audience—not to mention the thrill of a standing ovation—truly makes it all worthwhile. When you are acting, you are out of your life, thinking only about the character and the story, leaving no room to think about the worries and stresses of your day-to-day life. Nothing creates confidence like a job well done.

I love the quote from Agnes De Mille that says, "When you perform ... you are out of yourself—larger and more potent, more beautiful. You are for minutes heroic. This is power. This is glory on earth. And it is yours, nightly." This feeling can come from anything for which you have a passion. During Dr. Garfield's experience with the Apollo mission, the team labored long hours in poor conditions for little pay, working with a passion to bring about what will always be recognized as a historic, nearly unbelievable, even magical, achievement.

Mary Tanner, a career development specialist, newspaper columnist, and the author of *Managing from the Heart,* asks how many of us manage our careers from the heart. She says that we are all born with innate talents and abilities—we just weren't given an owner's operating manual. She encourages her readers to find activities they enjoy, even if they're not compensated for taking part in such activities.

You can do the same. Find the activities that bring out the kid in you. "Recognizing your lifestyle can help you zero in on the most satisfying way to earn a living", Tanner says. "Once you have examined your life and discovered your passion, consider what product or service might be a natural outgrowth of it." She gives some examples: "If you love gardening, teach others your techniques or sell a line of gardening tools. If hiking is your thing, plan outdoor adventures for companies or sell hiking gear."

In her book she includes a checklist that asks, among other things, the following questions:

- Is your product or service an extension of who you are?
- What makes you qualified to represent this product or service?
- What led you to the product or service you offer?

By taking time to study your lifestyle and joys, you will be able to identify your strengths, learn how to leverage and market your strengths, and live your life doing something you love. Find your passion, discover your mission, and visualize what brings you bliss—then get on with the show.

In theater, the cast creates the mission, which is usually obvious: create a successful show to entertain audiences. With this vision in mind, each actor then examines the goals and values that he will bring to his character. This activity is sometimes done in a group setting and sometimes alone. Here are some of the questions the actor considers: *What do I want my character to communicate to the audience? What is important to this character? What are this character's goals and values?* The actor then explores what behaviors should be exhibited on stage so that the audience will understand the values and belief systems of this character.

I remember a part I enjoyed in the show *Harvey*. You may remember the show—it's about a big rabbit that was invisible to all except Elwood P. Dowd. I played Veta Louise Simmons, Elwood's sister. She was worried about her brother, yet also concerned about how his strange behavior would look to the community. Veta possessed strong emotions and held tightly to her values. She loved Elwood and truly wanted to help him, yet at the same time he embarrassed her, and she wanted him out of the way—at least until her daughter's big party was over. So she decided to visit the local hospital for the insane to have Elwood committed. As she went through the interview, she explained how her brother constantly interacted with a giant rabbit whose name was Harvey. The doctor, beginning to question Veta's sanity, started making plans to commit her instead of Elwood. The more questions the doctor asked, the more frustrated Veta got, until finally she started to scream, rant, and rave like someone possessed.

When I played Veta, my challenge was to understand all of the emotions, values, and belief systems that Veta had acquired throughout her lifetime. I had to make the audience feel what she was feeling and to make them understand that she was acting simultaneously out of love for and allegiance to both Elwood and her daughter, yet also out of insecurity and embarrassment. But I couldn't give any of this information to the audience in so many words. I had to figure out how a person who was carrying all this baggage would behave in the situations portrayed in the play. This is the hardest part of acting: becoming the character.

Mentally, I examined Veta's background and childhood. What did she experience in her various roles as sister, mother, caregiver, and community leader? What did she feel in those roles? What was important to her? What were her core values—family, honesty, social status, financial security? What was her mission in life? Only after I had a full and clear understanding of who Veta was could I exhibit behavior and actions on stage that would communicate the essence of her character to the audience.

Bringing a character to life is a challenge that an actor faces with each new show and in each new role. Understanding the vision, values, and goals of a character is crucial to bringing that character to life for the audience. And practicing this skill in the pretend world of the theater makes it so much easier to do the same thing in real life. In theater, most of the background information is created in the actor's mind, as fantasy. That's why different actors have different interpretations and why you might see two actors perform the same role in two completely different ways, giving the same character a different personality each time.

Looking inward in real life, of course, is much more challenging. Discovering the values that are most important to you in your working life and your personal life requires time, patience, and—sometimes most of all—guts.

The first step to developing your mission or vision is to identify your core values. Only after that can you truly establish your goals. The behaviors that define your goals then become clear, and your action plan will follow. And once you've accomplished all this, writing the few sentences of a mission statement becomes easy. We'll talk more about goal setting and planning later, but for now, know this: nothing concrete happens without a mission or a long-term vision.

What is your personal mission? Does your company have a mission? Does everyone know it and contribute to accomplishing it? During the Apollo mission, the scientists, ordinary people working on an extraordinary project, had no certainty that they would succeed, but they had a burning desire—a passion for a successful mission. Driven by their passion, they achieved one of the greatest scientific accomplishments of the twentieth century. Their vision of success, of men walking on the moon, kept them going despite every obstacle.

What keeps you going? To be successful in business and in life you must have a clearly articulated mission that is fueled by your passion to succeed. Your mission is your long-range vision for yourself or for your business. "Leaders take responsibility for creating and communicating a clear vision," says the Disney organization in its Disney Institute training program. It goes on to say that "[a] *vision* is a picture of the future that is created in the imagination and [that] motivates employees to action. A *vision statement* is a collection of words, created collaboratively, that summarizes what an organization is intended to look like. Its purpose is to provide focus and serve as a reminder of where the organization is going. It helps to keep focus on the strengths of the company."

Success requires a clearly
articulated mission fueled by a
passion to succeed.

Actor's Critical Tip

It is not enough to have a mission statement that is on the wall for all to see. The mission must be part of all that the company and its employees live daily. But for a mission statement to do this, it must truly capture what is central to the organization and the reason for the organization's existence. Because of this, creating a personal or corporate mission statement will take some time and thought; spend about thirty minutes each day working on it until your mission and vision become clear.

Examples of effective mission statements:

Walt Disney World's Vision Statement: "Walt Disney World will always be dedicated to making dreams come true. In this magical world, fantasy is real and reality is fantastic. A wonderful sense of community waits, where all are greeted as welcome guests, and become cherished friends. For all who work and play here, Walt Disney World will be a source of joy and inspiration." The mission—'Keep the Magic Alive.'"

Ritz-Carlton: "We're ladies and gentleman serving ladies and gentleman."

Microsoft: "Our vision," says Bill Gates "is very simple. It's a computer at every desk, in every home, running Microsoft software."

Southwest Airlines: "The Mission of SWA is dedication to the highest quality of customer service delivered with a sense of warmth, friendliness, individual pride, and company spirit."

Some mission statements are better than others. When you create your mission statement, avoid making vague and meaningless statements or claims that cause your customers to comment, "Well, I should hope so."

For example, a well-known airline that shall here remain nameless has the following mission statement: "To build together the world's most preferred airline with the best people, each committed to exceeding our customer's expectations every day." Well, I should hope so! What are they supposed to say—"To build together the world's worst airline with incompetent, rude employees, each committed to meeting our customer's expectations regarding the horrors of air travel?"

This is why it is vital to define the core values that drive you and your business *before* you write your mission statement. If these values truly reflect who you are and what you want your business to achieve, then— and only then—your mission statement will be an accurate, sincere reflection of what you are trying to accomplish and bring to your customers.

TIPS AND TOOLS

Creating a mission statement

I've detailed some techniques and suggestions for creating a mission statement for an organization or for creating a personal mission statement. For the purposes of this material, we'll use the words *individual* and *organization* or *business* interchangeably.

Franklin Covey has a system it uses to develop a mission or vision. Covey's system offers classes whose details are also outlined in the popular Time Management and Planning system sold in Covey stores. The TMP system teaches that a mission statement describes your unique purpose in life. It captures the qualities you want to develop, the things you want to accomplish, and the contributions you want to make.

A personal mission statement becomes a guide for your life, inspiring you to make the decisions that will best help you reach your goals and fulfill your vision. Start by asking yourself the following questions:

- What will bring me happiness?
- How do I want to be remembered?
- What do I want people to say about me?
- What are some of my talents?
- What has been a defining moment in my life?
- What contributions do I want to make during my lifetime?

By answering these types of questions, you begin to get a sense of who you are and what is important to you. You uncover your core values, the things that are your very essence.

The Covey system helps you define your values, and your values influence how you make decisions. Your governing values reflect

- What is important to you
- How you see the world
- What you believe in

What is a mission statement or vision?

A mission statement states who and what you are and what you do, as well as how you'll be doing it. Your mission statement is a headline about your organization: *What it is we're here to do.*

It is a statement that tells the world how your organization is different or special, in your mind, from the rest of the world.

A vision statement describes what you want to be. It is future-focused. Your vision is your overall guiding direction.

How to create your mission statement
and vision statement

1. Identify the words or values that describe the character of your organization. What words come to mind when you want to describe your or your company's personality?
2. Ask key questions:
   - What is our business?
   - Who are our customers?
   - What value do we bring to our customers?
   - What do we do better than anyone else?
   - What makes us different or unique?
   - What are our guiding values or our driving forces?

A mission statement tells you where you are going; values and behaviors based on those values get you to where you are going. Once the values are clear, your mission flows from your values. Your daily behaviors and activities must match your mission and values. Examples of core values can include honesty, integrity, ethical behavior, courtesy, respect, fairness, professionalism, friendliness, helpfulness, commitment to team or family, continuous growth or improvement, excellence, and customer service.

3. Get input from others (employees, managers, and family members) with whom you work and live to make sure you include every important value required to create a shared vision.
4. Think about the future—say five years out—to start. Your organization has met its goals. What will it look like? What are others saying about you? How is your company operating? Are employees working as a team? Will you recognize and celebrate success when you see it? Will you reward it when it happens?
5. What do we need to do to accomplish our mission? In particular, what changes do we need to make?
6. Begin by
   - Generating a list of core values
   - Selecting ten

- Prioritizing the ten
- Reducing the list to five or less core values

7.   And then creating a mission statement of thirty-five words or fewer.

Your mission statement will be based on the core values shared by all in your organization. But just knowing your values isn't enough. To take things to the next level, identify the behaviors that support the values that support your mission. What are the critical success factors or critical steps that you must accomplish if you are to achieve your mission? For instance, if core values include customer service and professionalism, decide, what do customer service and professionalism look like? Perhaps they include behaviors such as smiling, shaking hands, greeting customers by name, and escorting customers to their destinations.

For example, I recently worked with an employee team to help them create a customer service mission statement. The team followed the procedure outlined above, gaining input from all owners, managers, and employees. They created their mission statement and vision, and they identified the core values vital to the organization, defining each. Finally, they established behaviors that were simple to recognize, easy to adopt, and that reflected what they wanted their customers to know about them. They laid all this out on a 2-inch by 6-inch trifold card and gave one to each employee to carry. Now the management judges employees by how well they adhere to the tenets of the mission and value statements.

In creating their mission statement and value statement, the team used the Ritz-Carlton model. Ritz-Carlton's simple but effective mission says, "We are ladies and gentlemen serving ladies and gentlemen." Ritz-Carlton employees follow what the company calls its Gold Standards:

- Credo
- Motto
- Three Steps to Service
- Twenty Basics

The Ritz-Carlton Credo defines what the company wants to accomplish: providing genuine care, offering the finest service and facilities available, creating an ambience suitable to every guest, and fulfilling the unexpressed wishes and needs of each guest. Ritz-Carlton employees say, "When in doubt, refer to the Credo."

The Ritz-Carlton Motto governs employees' actions and defines who they are. The Three Steps to Service are the three rules that guide each employee's behavior during a guest's stay: use the guest's name, anticipate the guest's needs, and give the guest a warm good-bye. The Twenty Basics are standards, behaviors, and tools that help each employee achieve the company's goals by implementing the Three Steps to Service.

Each employee carries a laminated card detailing all of the above. Ritz-Carlton employees and managers live their mission and train on it daily. If you have a Ritz-Carlton in your area, I suggest that you hold a training session there. The company often offers tours and training to businesses that are interested in learning the Ritz-Carlton philosophy.

I have been talking a lot about "appropriate behaviors." It is important to understand that these behaviors must be defined by managers and employees as they apply to their respective businesses. For instance, at Southwest Airlines, appropriate behaviors might include flight attendants telling jokes or singing songs. Shorts and miniskirts are considered appropriate dress. At most other airlines, however, such behavior and dress would likely be considered inappropriate by management. At the Pike's Place Fish Market, throwing fish to the customer is appropriate and encouraged—though in most retail stores, throwing the product to the customer would be frowned upon. You get the idea.

Each business must define what appropriate behavior looks like in its unique environment, and each individual should do the same. Everyone needs to be on the same page so that behaviors can be consistent throughout the company in focusing on providing desired levels of service.

Write your own obituary or eulogy

Another useful tool can be the writing of your own obituary or eulogy. Did you ever read *The Adventures of Tom Sawyer*? You may recall how Tom Sawyer and Huckleberry Finn secretly attended their own funeral and heard what people had to say about them and their lives. Consider: What might your obituary say? What eulogies might be given for you? Thinking about how you want to be remembered can help you identify the core values that reflect who you are. Do you want your obituary to read, "He was a workaholic," "She spent every weekend working," "He never took a vacation," or "She was a stranger to her children because her job came first"?

Take an honest look at yourself, both in your professional and your personal life, and identify where you want your life to take you. Identify the values that drive you, and ask yourself whether your behaviors reflect your values and your mission in life. Capitalize on your strengths—not your weaknesses—and then evaluate those areas of strength. The process of finding your bliss will be a creative one. It will build confidence and fuel your fire.

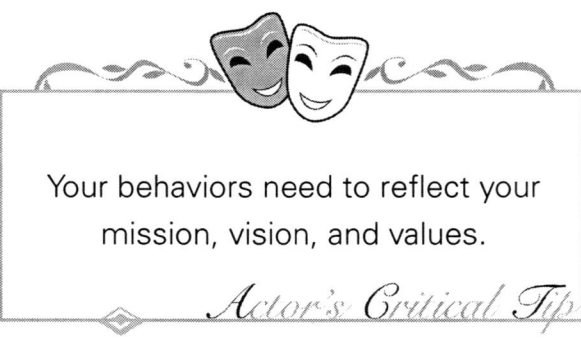

Your behaviors need to reflect your
mission, vision, and values.

Actor's Critical Tip

It will be time well spent. You will learn much about yourself that will make your life richer. And in the process of creating your mission and vision, you will discover your PASSION.

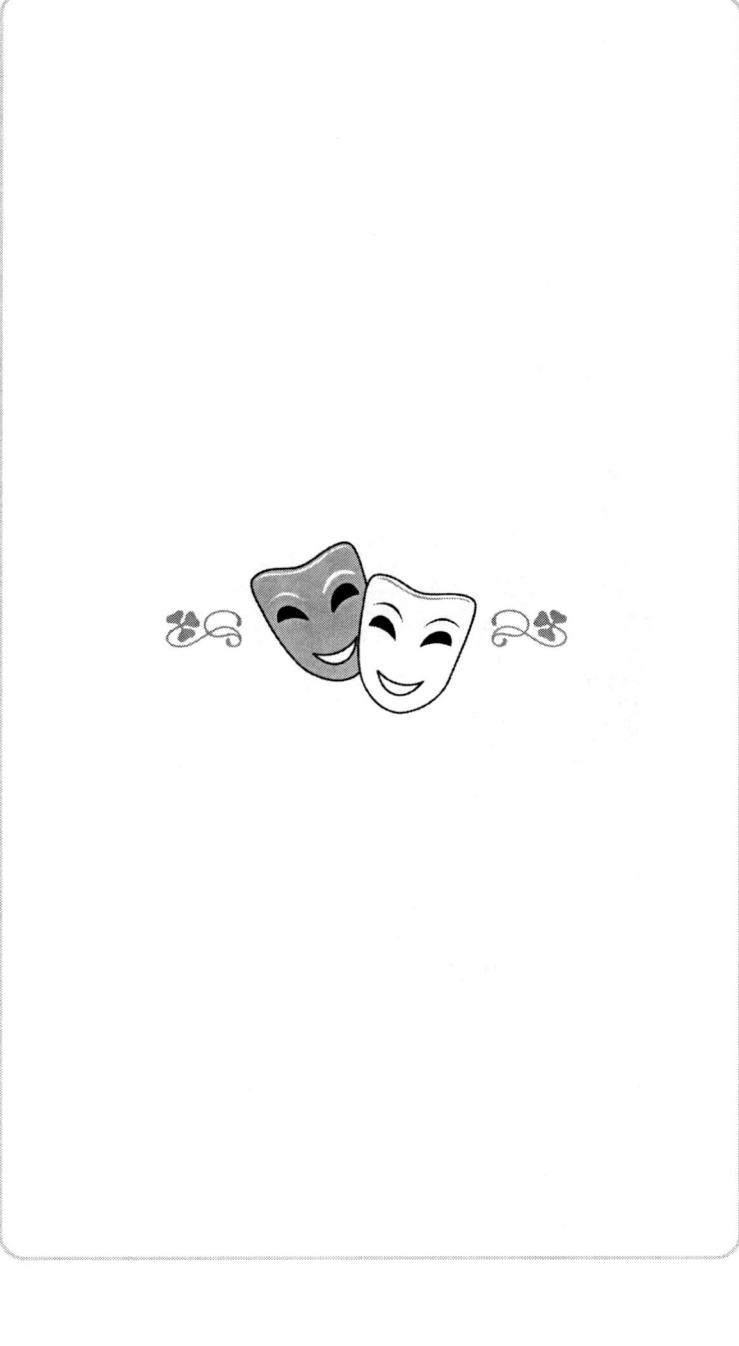

Together,
Wherever
We Go

TEAM WORK

Chapter 3

Wherever we go, whatever we do, We're gonna go through it together

Teamwork

("Together, Wherever We Go" from *Gypsy* —Lyrics by Steven Sondheim)

There is no more effective team than a cast of dedicated actors preparing for and performing a show. The interaction between cast members, the support they give to each other, and the feeling of oneness that arises from it all are incredible. In this chapter, you will read about examples of how a good cast operates as a well-oiled machine—as a team.

The parallels to the business world will be evident. The cast is like a team of employees or a department. The cast members are the employees, managers, and business owners. This chapter will describe how everyone in the organization can work together to put on a great show. The results everyone desires—great customer service, increased sales, and profits— can be attained when everyone works together to act as a cohesive entity. I'll share tips and tools for fostering team spirit, developing team building skills, and setting up effective teams within the organization.

Merriam-Webster's Dictionary defines a team as "[a] group of people working together toward a common goal." A cast getting together to put on a show is the epitome of the word *team*. Over about eight weeks, a group of strangers must become a single unit working together to create a show that earns rave reviews and standing ovations. How do they do it?

Much of the success depends on the leadership of the director. (We'll explore the leadership skills the director employs in detail in chapter five, when we talk about leadership.) To produce a good show, you have to start with the right team—the group of actors who together have the skills needed to get the job done. After the cast is assembled, the real work begins. The first thing the cast does is the read-through, which is just that: a reading of the script. The read-through gives the cast a high-level or big picture view of what the play is about.

Before anything else, it is important that everyone have the same vision of the desired outcome for the play. Although each individual cast member will create their own vision of their character, the overall vision or message of the show must be owned by each member from the beginning. Achieving this unity of aim is the first step in creating a high-performing team.

Next, each actor learns his part. And, yes, this is the part of the process most actors hate the most. It requires hours of memorization—hours and hours of it. But only after an actor has learned his lines perfectly can he begin to find his character. There is a wonderful time during the rehearsal process when everything clicks: the lines are memorized, and you can begin to develop the essence of your character.

The stages that both the play and the cast go through are exciting. The actors and the director push themselves and each other to do the play better, to do it differently, to make it more and more their own each time they rehearse. They are challenged to dig deep and find even more depth to bring to their characters. And the actors do not really come together as a team until they know their lines and their blocking (where to stand when delivering a line). Then they can begin to play off one another. This is the point when each actor can really listen to what each other actor is saying and gauge their reactions accordingly. And it is here that additional team members are added. They are the crew—the supporting cast—and no show can go on without them. One crew member is in charge of lighting, another does sound, and some build the set. Others make sure the props are gathered and moved on and off the set as needed.

This brings us to another very important team member—the stage manager. When the show opens, the director hands control over to the stage manager, who oversees and manages each performance.

Then the day arrives, and before you know it, opening night is here. Before each show, the team comes together for circle. Each theater company or director has a chosen method for circle, but the goal is the same each time: to get the cast and crew together about fifteen minutes before the show begins. During this time, some casts say a prayer; others do exercises to build energy, make announcements, recount stories, or thank one another for doing something that helped the cast or the play. There are many versions of circle, but each brings the team together to support each other and to support their common goal of putting on a memorable show that will entertain and move their audience.

During the performance, the team continues their support of each other. This is live theater—there are no do-overs. If someone forgets a line, another cast member jumps in to save him—and usually the audience has no idea that something went wrong. Actors are extremely grateful to other cast members who support them on stage and are always ready to reciprocate. Or, if the crew messes up—say, a phone doesn't ring or a doorbell is silent—the cast must save the day.

For example, in one show I did, I was supposed to turn on a radio and dance with my stage husband. We entered the scene, and I went to the radio and turned the dial. But something went wrong in the sound booth, and no sound came from the radio. When something like this happens, as any actor knows, your heart stops—but you must stay cool. So I turned to my husband and said, "I can't get this to work. Can you?" The dirty look he gave me was not part of the scene. He slowly walked toward the radio, played with the dial, and suddenly there was music. All the stalling we had done had given the sound technician enough time to fix the problem. That's live theater! So after that night, we came up with a

Plan B: if the sound didn't come on, one of us would hum, and we would dance as directed.

This is just one example of many I could share in which team members supported each other, and it also illustrates the importance of having a contingency plan in place. In a cast, the actors put great trust in each other. When I'm on stage, I always know that someone has my back, and that is very comforting.

The most impressive example of this was when I worked with a professional theater company in Orange County, California. This was a very talented group of actors, most of whom were educated or trained in theater. The play was an ensemble piece with most of us playing multiple roles. During one matinee performance, we were called on stage by the stage manager thirty minutes before curtain. She told us that one of the actors had taken ill and could not perform. "What shall we do?" she asked.

Immediately two of the most seasoned actors took control and asked who in the cast could do the roles. Four of the men volunteered, and we executed Plan B. Within ten minutes we had rehearsed the scenes. Then the costume people made some adjustments, and scripts were given to the actors. When this happens in theater, the audience is told that the actors filling in will use scripts onstage. The show went off without a hitch. The actors filling in did a great job of acting the parts, even with scripts in their hands, and the rest of the cast did all we could to support them, making sure they knew entrances, exits, and blocking. It was wonderful to watch this cast come together as a team to illustrate the well-known saying that the show must go on.

Another great lesson is that in theater we always take the time to thank each other for the support we give one another. Sometimes we do this over a drink or a bite to eat after the show. We all get together and laugh about the bloopers and, more important, the saves that happened on stage. Actor Tim Burton said it well: "We have laughed together, we have cried together. We have supported each other and learned from one another. We have become one amongst ourselves and with our audience. We have achieved unity. This is the glory of our art."

In a humbling process after the glow of success, the cast is usually required to stay after the last show to break down the set, clean the dressing rooms, put props and costumes back where they belong, and get the stage, backstage, and dressing rooms ready for the next cast.

Just as important is the celebration of success. When a team comes together to produce a wonderful show that earns rave reviews and encore performances, that team celebrates success together. After the run is over, there is almost always a cast party. We come together to bask in the success of the show and to thank each other for being a team that worked together, and won together, to create a work of art.

We have laughed together. We have cried together. We have supported each other and learned from one another. We have become one amongst ourselves and with our audience. We have achieved unity. This is the glory of our art.

—Tim Burton

Actor's Critical Tip

I read a quote from the famous football player Mike Singletary. He said it wonderfully when he said, "On a team, everybody has to be involved. There can't be any deadweight. It's too heavy. It's too costly. On a team, if one person comes up just a little bit short, everyone else has to step in to fill the gap. On a team, if someone has a problem, it becomes everybody's problem. If we are ever to get to the point where we think the person next to us, or the person under us, or the person over us, is not important, we'll come crashing down, no matter how high we fly."

I hope it has become obvious to you how the skills of the cast and crew who create a show can be translated into creating high-performing teams off stage.

What do all high-performing teams have in common? Frank Turek of the Austin Group in Launching and Leading a High Performance Team gives the following synopsis:

High-performance teams

1. Have a clear direction (goal)
2. Trust one another
3. Have a personal desire to achieve team goals

High-performing team members

1. Strive toward a common mission and are playing for high stakes
2. Let nothing stand in the way of the mission
3. Follow procedures, but with personal pride and style
4. Learn their role as well as those of the other players
5. Earn trust through integrity and professionalism
6. Are loyal and accountable to one another and their team leader
7. Serve others, regardless of rank, willingly sharing in the dirty work
8. Refuse to become complacent—they channel fear into focus
9. Recognize all others who contribute to the mission's success
10. Meet change and adversity with optimism and determination
11. Share a passion for service, accomplishment, and excitement
12. Achieve greatness by sacrificing comfort for service and growth

On what kind of team do you play? Is it a sports team, a work team, a family team?

Coming together is a beginning.
Keeping together is progress.
Working together is success.

Actor's Critical Tip

As a leader of a team, you can use tactics that will inspire success. Share information with your team. Communicate your group's common vision and mission. Communicate drivers of success and barriers to success that the team must overcome. Remember that good team leaders ask for input from other team members whenever possible. It is important that each team member knows what her role is on the team—or, better yet, her role in the show. Ask how each team member can support the others, and in doing so the common goal. Welcome all ideas, no matter from whom, and brainstorm solutions to problems and barriers. Good team leaders challenge the other members of their teams to stretch themselves and to develop new skills that will help the team accomplish its goals. Think outside the box as a leader—and as a team member—and have courage to try something new.

The thing about putting on a show is that each part of the experience is just plain *fun*. Accordingly, make it fun to be on the team. Encourage funny—even outrageous—ideas and brainstorm ways to make them work. Encourage creativity and innovation, and reward them when people exhibit them.

As a team player, do your part well and support the other members of your team, recognizing and thanking them whenever possible. Make your own individual commitment to the group effort. Make common ground with your teammates, finding something to share and talk about and work toward. Doing so will bring you closer together and help you create the result each of you wants.

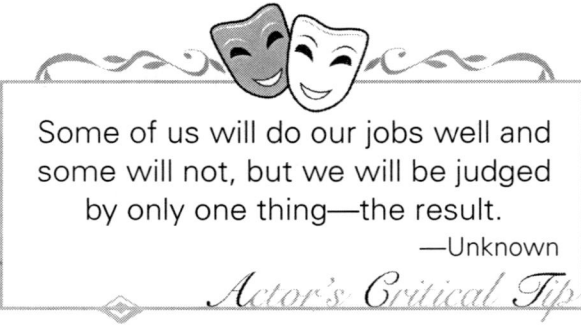

Some of us will do our jobs well and some will not, but we will be judged by only one thing—the result.

—Unknown

Actor's Critical Tip

The only way a team or organization succeeds is with the combined effort of each individual.

TIPS AND TOOLS

Create a team contract

Your team contract should be a one-page statement that clarifies your common goal and helps team members decide what needs to be done to accomplish the goal. The contract holds each team member accountable for doing his part. How will the team work together toward the common goal? Will the team have a leader or will it be self-directed? All team members must be involved in creating the contract, and all should sign it in agreement. Regularly review the contract and the behaviors it prescribes in support of the team goal.

Pick the right team members

Choose team members based on their knowledge, skills, and abilities to be sure the right person is in the right job.

Create an action plan

Your action plan should tell you what, who, when, and why:
What tasks are to be done?
Who will own each task?
When does the task need to be started? Completed?
Why are we doing this? What result or outcome do we expect?

Conduct a performance appraisal or debrief

Gather your team together for feedback from and to them.
Provide coaching where needed.
Ask the questions:
Did the team members achieve the team's goal?
Did the team members work together?
Did the team members develop and exhibit new skills or behaviors?
Did the organization benefit from what the team accomplished?
How did team members handle conflicts?
What part of our process do we need to keep, chuck, or create?
How will we celebrate our success?

Use LBNT

A good future-focused feedback and coaching technique I use often is called LBNT. I ask the person, "What did you like best about your performance? It is difficult to get people to say good things about themselves, so insist. I then tell them what I liked best. Then ask, "What would you do differently next time?" This keeps the focus on future improvement. Then I share what I think they could do to achieve a different and perhaps better result.

Can you relate to the following parable?

"That's Not My Job"
Once there were four people named Everybody, Somebody, Anybody, and Nobody. There was an important job to be done, and Everybody was sure that Somebody would do it. Anybody

could have done it, but Nobody did it. Somebody got angry about that because it was Everybody's job. Everybody thought Anybody could do it, but Nobody realized that Everybody wouldn't do it. It ended up that Everybody blamed Somebody when Nobody did what Anybody could have.

—Author unknown

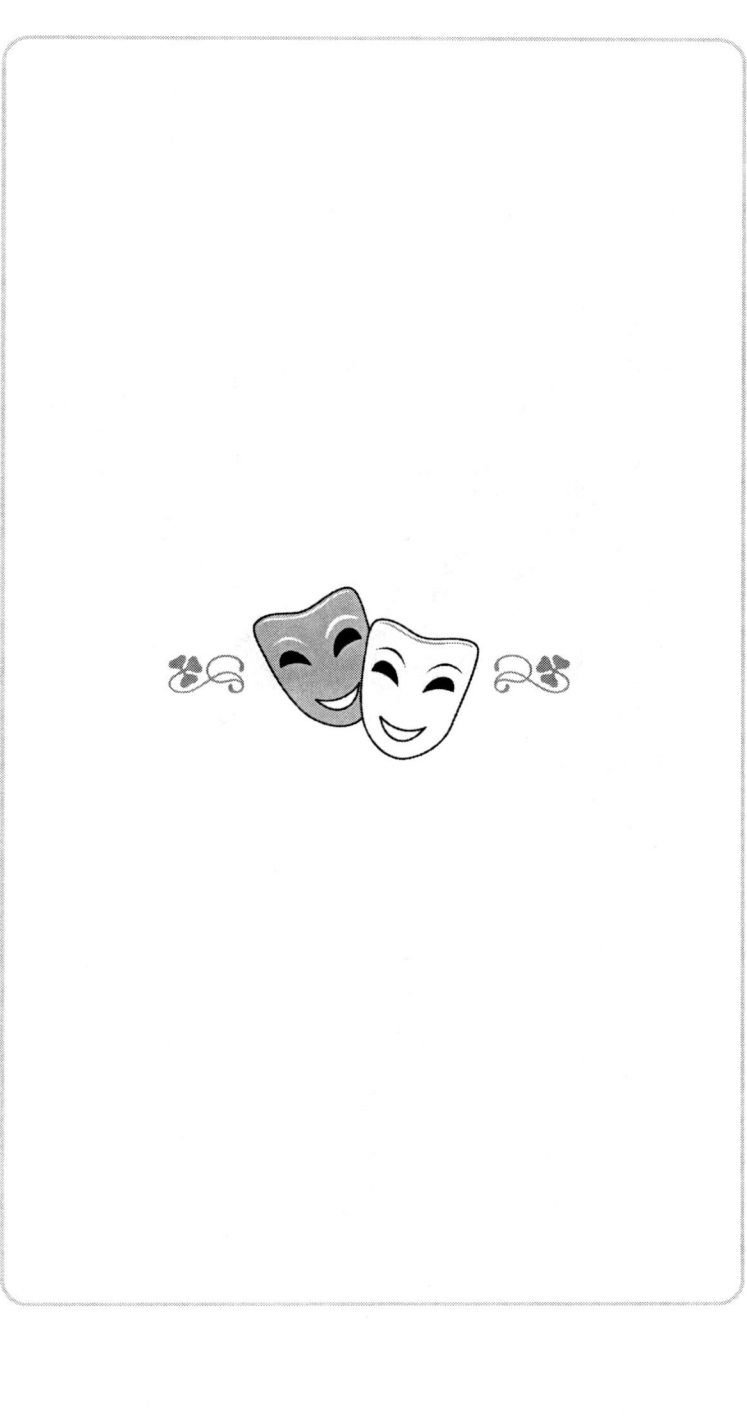

Climb Every Mountain

GOAL - SETTING SKILLS

Chapter 4

Climb ev'ry mountain, Ford every stream, Follow every rainbow, Till you find your dream

Goal-Setting Skills

("Climb Ev'ry Mountain" from *The Sound of Music*
Lyrics by Oscar Hammerstein II)

It is impossible to get where you are going if you do not know where it is that you are going. After all, any road will do if you are uncertain about your destination. Having a goal that is clear—and in writing—is crucial for success.

In business, we talk about SMART goals: goals that are Specific, Measurable, Attainable, Realistic, and Timely. Such goals are fundamental for anyone reaching toward her potential. The same sorts of goals are also used in theater by the actors and the director as they work to put a show together. My goal now is to challenge you to set goals for yourself. I will also offer you a plan for reaching your goals. You will understand the importance of setting goals and developing action plans, whether as an employee, a manager, a supervisor, or any other individual trying to achieve professional or personal goals.

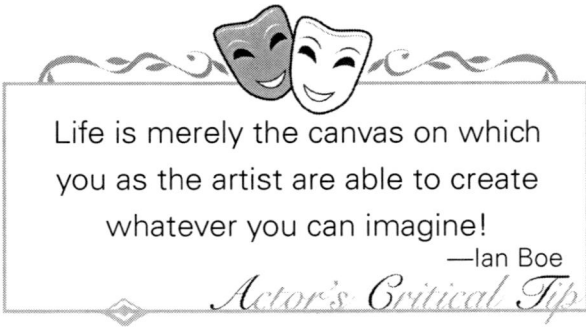

Life is merely the canvas on which you as the artist are able to create whatever you can imagine!
—Ian Boe

Actor's Critical Tip

In theater the goal is obvious—to produce a great show. This goal is a SMART goal. It is **Specific** (putting on the show [the what] and putting it on well [why], by relying on the team mission statement and vision [how]), and it is **Measurable** (which is important—because if you can't measure it, you can't manage it).

In theater, there are many short-term measurements, such as the date to be off book (having lines memorized), the date for all costumes and makeup to be finalized, and the date for tech week (commonly known as "hell week"), the week before opening when all the technical details such as lighting, sound, music, and blocking are finalized. The criteria for these measurable goals are what should be accomplished, what the end result will look like, and in what timeframe all this is going to happen.

Our goal is also **Attainable**. We ask ourselves, "Can we do it? Is it realistic? Can we accomplish it with the people we have and within the timeframe we've set?" (Some experts say the A in SMART goals can also mean **Aligned**. Is the goal aligned with the mission, vision, and values of the organization? For example, some theaters do only children's theater; others remain in one genre or appeal to a certain audience.)

We also need to choose a **Realistic** goal. Do we have the skills and talent to pull it off? Are our timeframes realistic? (This does not necessarily mean easy; the group should be challenged, and the bar set high—but within the bounds of possibility.) Our last criterion is **Timely**. We give ourselves a timeframe for completion. In theater, this is opening night.

The director reviews the SMART goals to ensure that the cast has a complete understanding of the goal. One terrific director I will always remember personifies the good leader I describe later, when we talk about leadership: Terri Miller-Schmidt. Terri's style of leadership and the way she sets goals exemplify how things should be done. When she directed *To Kill a Mockingbird* for the Old Town Theater in Temecula, California, the cast was a large one, featuring all ages, from young kids and teens to adults and older adults, too. I played the oldest cast member, Mrs. Dubose, who was very old and very sick. My role—like all the other roles—was challenging. *To Kill a Mockingbird* is an iconic show; one of our goals was to make it our own, not merely a replica of the stage show or the movie.

Terri's work with this cast was fascinating to observe. Most actors know that the hardest actors to play against are children and animals. I have been in shows before with children and teens; if the director does not set and enforce goals, absolute chaos can ensue, creating a stressful experience for all involved. When I saw the number of child and teen actors in the show, I was apprehensive, but Terri took control from the start. First, with her goal of creating a memorable performance in the forefront of her mind, she chose her cast well. She put the right people in the right roles, people who had the talents and skills she desired to make her goal attainable. She gave us the time we needed to learn our lines and become comfortable with our characters. And when we were ready, she added another layer to our characters, adding dimension to them and measuring the result against the results she was looking for.

For example, my character's sickness made her mean and angry. When Terri was satisfied that I had mastered mean and angry in addition to old and sick, she said, "Now add disappointment to her." When she was satisfied with my injection of disappointment into Mrs. Dubose, she told me, "Good job. You gave me what I asked for. Now add sadness." She told me that my goal should be to make the audience feel for Mrs. Dubose and empathize with her, instead of just hating her for being so mean to the children. I had to keep that goal in mind as I developed my character.

Terri used this technique with each cast member, measuring his performance and adding another specific characteristic only when she was confident that the actor was ready for the next level toward achieving the team's goal. As each of us mastered the different levels or emotions for our character, Terri challenged us with something else to think about. Terri was acutely aware of the skill level and potential of each actor. She challenged and pushed each of us until we reached our potential and attained the goal she had set forth in her mind as she examined the various characters in the play.

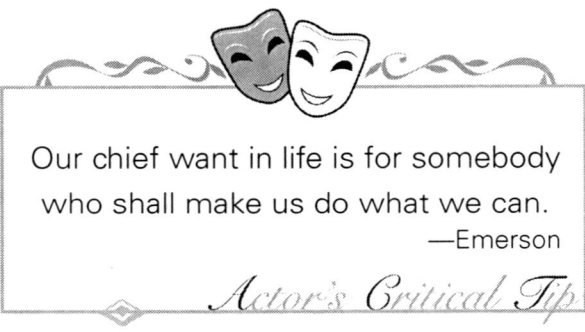

Our chief want in life is for somebody who shall make us do what we can.
—Emerson

Actor's Critical Tip

To keep us on track after each rehearsal, she gave us notes first, providing immediate feedback, praising our efforts and then issuing a new challenge. In the end, thirty-two actors performed a wonderful show with a professional and thoroughly impressive level of consistency and quality in each performance. As our leader, Terri directed us to be the best that we could be. She got us to rehearse for seven weeks, fifteen hours a week, with no financial gain for us personally. And Terri met her SMART goals. The show was a great one. It often sold out and always got a standing ovation. Terri was a no-nonsense leader who set clear goals, continually raising the bar and challenging the team to step up. And the level of dedication, persistence, and performance she encouraged in this cast would be welcomed by any manager of any business.

What is the lesson here for any leader? Hire right. Get the right people in the right job. I recommend the book *Good to Great* by Jim Collins, who says, "Leaders of companies that go from good to great start not with 'where' but with 'who.' They start by getting the right people on the bus, the wrong people off the bus, and the right people in the right seats." Only after this does a leader train the group to do what they need to do. Develop a team, and challenge them to meet their full potential. Recognize and reward the behaviors you are looking for in your team. Motivate your people to perform at higher levels to achieve their goals—not only for their own benefit, but for the good of the team or organization. If you can do that, your team will get tremendous applause, rave reviews, standing ovations, and a demand for encore performances from raving fans.

Let's explore this concept further in the business environment. We start with setting the goals and make sure they are SMART goals. Let's say the goal is Point B, the final destination and desired outcome. Yogi Berra said, "If you don't know where you are going, you will wind up somewhere else."

Once we know where we want to go, then where you are now is the starting point. Let's call it Point A. Why is this important? What if someone were to ask you, "How do I get to Los Angeles?" What would you tell him? Until you know the starting point of his journey, you can't tell him how to get to where he wants to go.

When you set goals, not only do you need to know your final destination (Point B), but you also must know where you are now (Point A). For instance, if you were in sales and set a goal of closing or selling to 50 percent of the people to whom you make a presentation, you first need to know what your closing ratio is today.

Once you have identified both Point A and Point B, the next step is to create an action plan to get you from your starting point to your goal. Another important step in this goal-setting process is to put your goals into writing. If something is not in writing, it is a wish, not a goal.

In Brian Tracy's book *GOALS!*, he references the book *What They Don't Teach You in the Harvard Business School*, in which author Mark McCormack tells of a study conducted of students in the 1979 Harvard MBA program. Students were asked if they had set clear, written goals for the future and had made plans about to how to accomplish them. Only 3 percent of the graduates had written goals and plans; 13 percent had goals, but not in writing; and a whopping 84 percent had no specific goals at all. Ten years later, the members of the class were interviewed again, and the findings were astounding—and predictable. The 13 percent of the class who'd had goals were earning, on average, twice as much as the 84 percent who'd had no goals at all. And the 3 percent who'd had clear, written goals were earning, on average, 10 times as much as the other 97 percent put together.

Tracy continued to explore why people do not set goals. In my experience, he is right on when he lists his top reasons—which also shed light on why people fail (something we'll explore in depth in chapter six, when we talk about risk and failure). People who do not set goals often lack knowledge of why goals are important. No one, whether parent, teacher, or coach, ever taught them the importance of setting goals. They don't even know how to set goals, and they certainly lack the knowledge of how to set SMART goals. Very often, people who do not set goals are afraid of failure—forgetting that you must risk failure on your way to success.

Yet another reason that people fail to set goals is that they fear rejection. They fear that if they don't meet their goals, they will be criticized, judged, and perhaps even punished. And I'll add one more: some people do not set goals because they fear success. As strange as such a thing may seem, some people are afraid that if they succeed, they will be forced to set another goal, one that may require them to work harder or longer than ever before.

Goal setting, like everything else, will become a habit when you practice it consistently. When you start to reach your goals and attain the positive results of achievement, setting additional goals becomes easier. As you develop more confidence in your ability to meet goals, this belief in your capabilities will govern the level of your performance. The more you believe in what you can do, the higher the goals you'll set.

Confident people persevere because they are absolutely committed—and they are more often those who succeed. Mastery of goal setting, like mastery of anything else, requires training, patience, persistence, and practice. But once you master goal setting and start to achieve success, you'll begin to believe that you can achieve anything. Success breeds confidence, and confidence breeds success. Just remember, if you never set a goal, you will never fail—but you will also never succeed.

TIPS AND TOOLS

Begin at the end—future focus

What is your goal? Where do you want to be? To begin setting goals, first do what Steven Covey suggests and begin with the end in mind. Ask yourself, "What will it look like? What will it feel like if I am successful? Where do I want to be? What do I want the outcome to look like? What is my goal?" If a newspaper were to write the story of your life and your accomplishments, what would it say? And what will achieving your goals bring you? Fame? Money? Status? Pride? What will your future look like? This end result, this outcome, this goal, is your Point B.

Where am I now?

Once you have envisioned what your end result will look like, determine where it is that you are now. What is your starting point? This, your current state, your present position, is Point A. For example, if your goal is weight loss, what do you weigh now? If you want to earn a certain amount of money per year, how much are you earning now? If you want to sell more of a product or service, how much are you selling now?

Action plan

How will I get from Point A to Point B? Develop an action plan laying out just this—in detail. Your action plan should include who, what, how, and when. Who will do what? How will she do this? When will it need to be done?

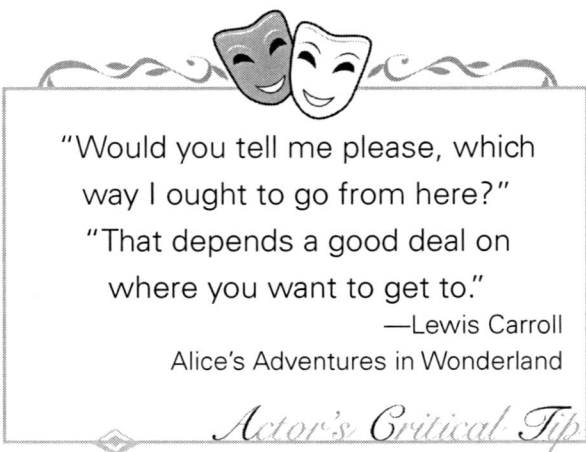

"Would you tell me please, which
way I ought to go from here?"
"That depends a good deal on
where you want to get to."
—Lewis Carroll
Alice's Adventures in Wonderland

Actor's Critical Tip

Put your goals in writing

If goals are not written down, your chances of success are reduced dramatically. You must commit yourself to succeeding. Be sure to write down your goals and review them every day. On the path to achieving your long-term goal, lay out interim goals to mark milestones in your progress toward your ultimate goal. The more discipline you have in writing down and reviewing your goals daily, the more you can convince yourself that you truly can achieve your goals—and thus the more willing you will be to stay on track in doing so. Visualize success daily, weekly, monthly, quarterly, yearly—until you have achieved it. Make lists to chart your path and progress: a master list, a monthly list, a weekly list, a daily list.

Identify barriers

Determine the barriers standing in the way of your success. What do you have to start, stop, or continue doing to be successful? (For example, to lose weight you must be willing to eat less and exert yourself more.) What skills do you need to develop to achieve success? What tasks will be required of you?

In his *Leadership* seminars on DVD, Brian Tracy quotes Jack Walsh, former CEO of General Electric, defining what he called "the reality principle" as the ability to see the world as it really is: to ask, "What's the reality?"

Peter Drucker called it "intellectual honesty: dealing with the facts exactly as they are, prior to attempting to solve a problem or make a decision."

Identify where you are today and what it is going to take to get you to where you want to be. Identify your critical success factors—the steps that you must complete if you are to be successful. Identify your strengths, along with the challenges that you'll face. Examine the processes, procedures, and practices necessary for you to do it right.

Do not be afraid to fail

Failure comes from not doing the things you know you must do to succeed. Successful people fail much more often than unsuccessful people. Research some of the great success stories, and you'll hear many stories of failure along the way. When Thomas Edison was asked how he felt about failing so many times before he succeeded in inventing the light bulb, he replied that he did not consider himself to have failed but rather to have discovered thousands of ways that would not work.

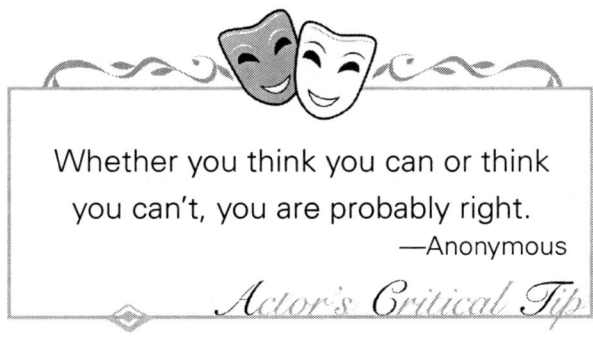

Whether you think you can or think you can't, you are probably right.
—Anonymous

Actor's Critical Tip

As the great coach Vincent Lombardi said, "A man can be as great as he wants to be. If you believe in yourself and have the courage, the determination, the dedication, the competitive drive—and if you are willing to sacrifice the little things in life and pay the price for the things that are worthwhile—it can be done."

Reevaluate if needed

At any time during your quest to meet your goal, feel free to reevaluate. Do you need to adjust your behavior or perhaps even your goals? Be honest in your evaluation. Make your goal attainable but also be honest about your commitment—and your discipline—to doing what you recognize you have to do to accomplish your goals.

Think in terms of behaviors: what would it look like?

Think about what you want to accomplish and about the values that define those accomplishments. Then identify behaviors that will manifest those values and accomplishments. Many people define behaviors using adjectives such as *unprofessional*, *sloppy*, or *lacking in integrity*. They might say of someone that "his behavior was unprofessional" or that "he needs an attitude adjustment." Instead, begin to define behaviors by how the desired outcome would look. What would it look like to be a professional? What are the behaviors of a professional? If someone observed another person behaving professionally, what is it that they would see? But also realize that professionalism might look different in different environments.

It is important to decide on the professional behaviors you want for your team or organization. In some cultures, a shirt and tie defines the professional look. In others, a shirt bearing a company name and the employee's name may be acceptable. What does having a high level of integrity or honesty look like? How are these values manifested in behaviors?

On a personal note, for example, suppose your goal is to become a loving spouse. Ask yourself or your partner what love looks like. Love might look like offering support when needed, actively listening, and spending time together.

When you know what something looks like and the behaviors that define it, that thing becomes much easier to accomplish. What behaviors, tasks, and physical manifestations are necessary to reach your goal and its desired outcome?

Celebrate success: reward and recognition

Remember to reward yourself and anyone else working toward the same goals. And keep in mind that there's a difference between reward and recognition. We'll explore this in chapter nine. For now, celebrate your success along the way to reaching your goals.

Author Jeff Olson said, "Successful people do what unsuccessful people are not willing to do, and that often means living outside the limits of one's comfort zone."

I think Johann Wolfgang von Goethe said it best: "Whatever you can do, or dream you can, begin it. Boldness has genius, power, and magic in it. Press on, my friends; your goals are right there within your reach."

LEADERSHIP SKILLS

Chapter 5

I can fly higher than an eagle, 'Cause you are the wind beneath my wings

Leadership Skills

("The Wind Beneath My Wings" — Sung by Bette Midler)

Would you believe that there exists a person who can bring a group of diverse and talented people together, motivate them to work as one team, willingly, in excess of twenty hours a week—without pay!— and achieve as the end result of their combined efforts a well-designed, impressive product that people will gladly pay to experience? What do you call this incredible leader who has the talents and skills to motivate a team to perform at their highest potential, for little or no pay, for hours on end? You call this leader a *director*.

It is with good reason that the Best Director award is presented at the height of any awards ceremony, right before Best Picture. This is because it is the director who makes the magic happen in theater, film, and television—in fact, in any entertainment medium. The director chooses his cast (team) and motivates them to perform, encouraging, critiquing, and making adjustments as needed, all while fixing mistakes, recognizing his cast for a job well done, and making all the key decisions—and the list goes on and on. The director is the one behind the scenes who the audience never sees. He is the glue that holds the production together. He is the catalyst of the end result, the product and service delivered—in other words, the show. How can one person make this happen?

I will never forget my first director: the late Ron Lieberman of Playhouse 22, East Brunswick, New Jersey. My first show was *Joseph and the Amazing Technicolor Dreamcoat*. I was cast in the chorus, mostly because they wanted my son Brian in the show. Brian was only about eight at the time; I was a pity cast to get Brian. It was my first stage experience, and I was very nervous. I was in awe of the talents and confidence of the other people who were cast. About half of the cast were experienced actors and the other half enthusiastic rookies, but I was the only one performing for the first time.

Ron started with the basics—a good technique—even with experienced people. He explained about staging and blocking, explaining theatrical terms like *upstage* and *downstage*—all the basic necessities needed for success. He then said something I will remember forever: "This show will only be as good as its weakest link. There are no small or insignificant parts or players within this cast or crew. The audience will see and react to the entire show, and they will notice the slightest flaw. If a spotlight is off-center or a cast member makes eye contact with the audience looking for friends or family, if the microphones do not work properly, if the music is off—these are the things the audience will notice and talk about. All the components need to work together—each and every one of you— to create a wonderful show for our audiences. You must work as a family works and love as a family loves so that your audience will feel and react to the love and symmetry of this family. Only then will magic happen."

Ron was right. We did as he directed, and the show was so magical that we had to add extra performances. After each show, some audience member always commented to a cast member that he or she could feel the love the cast had for each other and could sense how much we were enjoying putting on this show for the crowd. I have done countless shows since then and worked with some wonderful directors, and I have been privileged to have felt the magic many times. I will always remember Ron's words: "The show will only be as good as its weakest link."

I know Ron would agree with the quote, "There are no small parts, only small actors." There is some debate as to whether Stanislavsky Konstantin, creator of The Method, or Ed Wynn, the famous actor, said these words, but they hold true for me today as I perform on stage and in my professional life.

> The show is only as good
> as its weakest link.
> —Ron Leiberman, Playhouse 22
> East Brunswick, NJ
> *Actor's Critical Tip*

The principles and techniques of the great directors I have been privileged to work beside can be duplicated by a leader or manager in any workplace to produce similar results. The leadership role is paramount to a business success: a company rises and falls based on the effectiveness of its leader or leaders. When practiced by managers, the tools and techniques of the director can motivate employees toward optimum performance. Let's move on to take a look at some of these tools and how we can apply them to the world of business.

Effective leadership tools

- Hiring (casting)
- Motivating
- Training (rehearsing)
- Recognizing

Hiring

In the acting world, hiring, or casting, is relatively easy. All that is needed to bring thespians flocking to an audition is a notice in the paper, a flyer in the mail, or an announcement online. In the business world, however, things are more difficult. And whether plenty of people or few respond to an ad, the secret isn't getting the people to come: it's hiring the right people out of those who do come. The leaders of any business must develop tools to identify the qualities of the employees who are right for the company and then recruit those people, interview them well, and work hard to retain them.

To get the right people, first decide what the right people look like. What character traits are important? What skills or talents are needed? What type of person will fit into the culture of the business? Begin by listing these must-have traits.

Then determine what a particular person's job description will be. In the theater, as early as the audition, the candidate is given a character description. As an actor, it is easier to audition for a role when you understand the person whom you are portraying, and the same is true with employees. The subject of an interview, as well as the person interviewing her, can assess the suitability of a possible match much more easily if all parties know what is expected of the person who will ultimately fill the position. The tasks and responsibilities that compose the role should be well thought out and should be communicated during the recruitment and interview process. As John Clancy, founding artistic director of the New York International Fringe Festival, says, "The bottom line is that it's your job to directly ask for what you want from an actor and then get it on stage."

What's more, knowing the culture of your business and communicating it to applicants is vital for success. If your business is extremely customer-focused, recognize this and then look for matching traits in potential employees. A candidate who only wants to know how much money she can make working for you might not fit into the culture of such a business.

Just as the director chooses the entire cast based on talents and appearance, he or she also decides whether a particular actor will mesh with the other actors and whether he possesses the ability to see the big picture—the message the playwright is trying to send to the audience.

Ask yourself: "Does this candidate get it? Does she understand what this business is all about?" Jeremy Brock, a UK-based director, states, "As a director, your job is to articulate where you think [the cast] should be going, while at the same time making them feel that they own that [goal]. The actor has to own the performance. It's one of the things you have to learn to do: to guide an actor towards the performance you want without making them feel bullied."

In the same way, it takes a skillful interviewer and a well-thought-out process of recruiting and hiring to ensure that the right people are hired for the right jobs.

Motivating

In community theater, the actors are usually not paid. So how skillful does the director have to be to motivate the cast to rehearse upward of fifteen hours a week for six to eight weeks and then perform twelve to fifteen shows? In professional theater, the actor has to be able to sustain a character throughout rehearsal and through eight shows a week over a minimum of six to eight weeks—perhaps through the months, even years, of a long-running show. In a show I did many years ago, one actor continually asked the director after each directed action: "What is my motivation?" The director calmly took the time to talk to the actor about the reason for his direction to help the actor make sense of his character's actions. But after the fourth or fifth time the actor asked the question, the director curtly replied, "Do you want this part? If so, that is your motivation to do what I direct you to do."

As Jessica Kubzansky, the co-artistic director of Theatre@Boston Court in Pasadena, said in an interview, "If an actor of mine lost the quality required for the character that I saw originally, the first thing I do is have a conversation with him or her. We start by talking about the character and what the ideal world would be. Then we discuss where the character is at the moment. And often, once the actor has been made aware of [the problem], he or she is able to correct it or we work together to find out how to get there. In that conversation, oftentimes a light bulb goes off for the actor, and they are able to recapture—or, rather, newly, more fully create—the character."

As a leader, first be confident that your employee is well trained and informed and that he knows what and how things need to be done. Only then, if the person is still failing, ask the question both of yourself and him: why is he not doing what he knows needs to be done? This is a harder question to answer and one that in many cases is never asked; instead, the employee is terminated.

The answer is motivation. A successful person is one who is willing to do what an unsuccessful person won't do. Sometimes behavior does not change, even when you know how or why to do something, but it does change when standards are raised and the focus changed. We all know the description of one type of insanity: continuing to do the same thing while expecting different results.

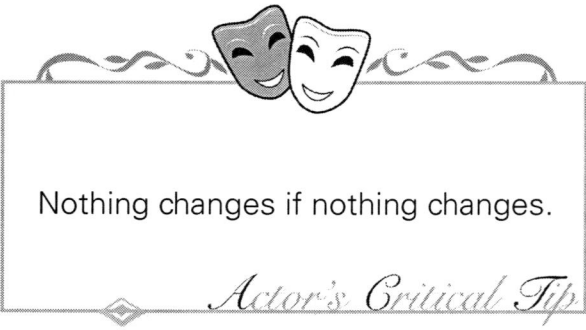

Nothing changes if nothing changes.

Actor's Critical Tip

This is why diet and exercise programs often fail: people know what to do and how to do it, but until they are motivated to make a change—until the focus shifts—change is elusive.

The challenging task for a leader is to find out what it will take to motivate a person to do what must be done to achieve success. Often, unfortunately, managers think money must be the answer, and they throw performance bonuses at their employees. Sometimes this works, but not always; and if money does not work, managers are often at a loss for what else to do. So how do you find out what motivates a particular employee? It's simple: ask him.

Often the reason that the prospect of increased salary or added bonuses does not work is that the employee cannot appreciate what he has not yet had. If an employee earns a decent salary and lives within his means on it, he may not be motivated to work harder or to change the way he works to earn more. (That is not to say that you can pay people less and pat them on the back instead. Your pay scale must be competitive to get the best employees. But, conversely, increases in pay will not keep an employee who feels unappreciated and is never recognized for a job well done.)

Try something interesting with an unmotivated employee: ask what she would do if she made an extra $2,000 this month. If she cannot answer you immediately, then money may not be the answer for this person—or else she may not have thought about what more money could be used for.

Tom Hopkins, my favorite sales trainer, tells the story of someone he hired to sell real estate. This person was doing all right but had the potential to do better; yet he was not motivated to work any harder. Tom asked the employee what he would do with $2,000. The employee replied that he would put a down payment on a boat. Tom marched the employee down to the local marine outfitter and had him pick out the boat of his choice and put a small deposit on it. Tom told the owner, and his employee, that the employee would be back in one month with the rest of the deposit and back in six months to pick up the boat. Do you think the employee was motivated now?

The moral is that it is not always the money that is the motivator but instead what the money represents to that employee and what dream it can buy for the employee and his family.

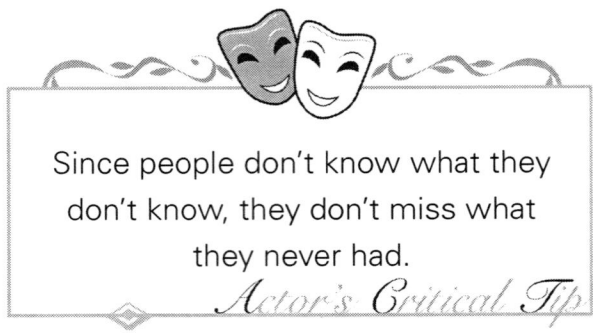

Since people don't know what they don't know, they don't miss what they never had.

Actor's Critical Tip

But what about the employee who is not motivated by the prospect of more money? Again, ask what motivates the person. Often, it is time. In today's very busy world, having more time for family and self is often a great motivator, and all the more so when many industries require long hours on the job. Perhaps a day off or the opportunity to leave work early will be all that it takes to motivate an employee to step up his game and do what it takes to bring management's goals to fruition.

So how can you keep employees motivated? Psychologist Dennis Waitley reminds us, "Everyone is motivated ... a little or a lot. What most managers mean is 'I wish my people were more motivated.'"

As I said earlier, just ask employees what motivates them. Joe Verde, an automotive sales trainer, suggests the following:

Hold a meeting and make two lists. Brainstorm everything the team can think of that motivates people: recognition, time off, more effective training, good managers, and so forth. On the next list, outline things that de-motivate people: long hours, ever-changing pay plans, poor or ineffective training, unsupportive managers, lack of recognition, and so on. Start implementing some of the things on the motivational list, phase out some of the things on the de-motivational list, and see what wonders happen. For more on motivation, rewards, and recognition, see the discussion of recognition later in this book.

Training

In theater, training is called "rehearsing." I'm sure you have heard this saying: it is not practice that makes perfect, but perfect practice that makes perfect. During rehearsals, the director encourages perfect practice. The actors do the scene over and over until it is perfect, then they lock it in and repeat it again and again until it looks unrehearsed and becomes a part of their nature.

In business, the leaders must do the same when providing the training that is needed for success. As a leader, it is your responsibility to be sure your employees have the skills and tools they need to be successful. In Cheryl Kimball's book *Horse Wise* she writes, "Leaders do not leave people wondering what to do next; they give them the tools they need to make good decisions and to be able to proceed with confidence. A good leader also lets people flounder around a little, searching for their own path to the answer they need—all the while knowing that the leader is there, aware of the situation and ready to step in and reassure or clarify when necessary." She goes on to say, "A good leader gains his or her role through respect. You can lead through dominance and fear, but that only creates negative feelings. Leadership through respect creates good feelings all around."

Remember the difference between feedback and input. Feedback is a gift—the employee can choose whether to act upon it. Input, however, is a directive: the employee should comply. Distinguish between the two when you give advice and give instructions so that there is no question about whether an employee has a choice about following your directions. Before you give your employees feedback, ask for their permission to do so. After you have given the feedback, ask them what they will do differently based on the feedback—but without making them feel as if you're just trying to get them to repeat your words back to you and act as your puppets. Keep your conversation about expectations, not about accusations. Director, author, and acting coach Kimberly Jentzen says, "A coach should criticize you, tough-love you at times, always encourage you and look for ways to make you smile. It's like having your own personal cheerleader inside your head, warm and supportive." I love Noel Coward's line: "I can take any amount of criticism as long as it is unqualified praise."

Recognizing

As mentioned earlier, for many, motivation comes in the form of recognition. I often say to managers that the difference between a pat on the back and a kick in the rear is only about six inches—but it is an important six inches, so stay above the line.

- Recognize and reward the members of your team. Recognition costs nothing, and it pays great dividends. Rewards are tangible tokens of your appreciation for a job well done.

- Provide incentives for excellent achievement. Pay for the performance you are looking for, and remember that WIIIFM (What Is In It For Me?) is always asked internally by someone who is asked to perform a task.

Rewards may be more tangible, but don't knock recognition. Recognition is so vital to the success of both individuals and businesses that we'll spend an all of chapter nine discussing it later.

TIPS AND TOOLS

Why do people fail?

People fail for two reasons:

1. Lack of Knowledge
2. Lack of Will

Lack of knowledge

Some people lack skills, knowledge, or the expertise to get the job done. Other people do not understand the importance, or priority, of their task or goal.

Action plans

Training

- Train your employees. You can't blame someone who hasn't been trained.

- Ask questions to find out what knowledge is lacking and train on those skills.

- Provide a suitable environment for success: tools, location, lighting, and equipment all play a part.

- Remove or reduce obstacles to success.

- Communicate to the failing employee the importance of doing what needs to be done in the appropriate way and within the appropriate window of time. Remember that it is not enough for an employee to merely hear; he must truly comprehend how to apply his knowledge and measure his success.

- Explain the importance and priority of accomplishing the chosen goal or task.

- Encourage the employee in effective ways.

- Measure and monitor the results of the employee's efforts.

- Recognize and reward the employee, celebrating his success.

Lack of will

Some people are not willing to do what they know how to do, and what they know they must do.

Action plans

Motivate

- Find out what motivates each individual, asking him what would motivate him to work harder or better. It might be any number of things—money, time with family, recognition for a job well done, or any number of other things. And when you suspect money is not a motivator, ask the Tom Hopkins question: "What would you buy today with $2,000?" If your employee has no ready answer, you know that money is not his motivation. Ultimately your employee must answer these questions for himself: Why is it worth my while to work hard? What am I willing to do to accomplish my goals? And when your employee has come to his own answers, talk with him to find out what they are.

Terminate

- When all else fails, ask yourself, "Is this the right employee in the right job?" If not, transfer the employee to a different position or terminate his connection with the company.

The presence of a good leader in both theater and business is the secret to success. In 2006 *Backstage Magazine* held a contest to identify the best acting teacher. Howard Fine of Howard Fine Acting Studio in Hollywood earned the most votes. Fine attributed his inspiration to the famous acting coach Uta Hagen, his mentor. Fine said, "She was never cruel, but extremely specific in the work. How can you not be inspired by someone who approached acting like a scientist, constantly trying to figure out how to make it better? You know the old saying, 'Those who can't do teach'? Uta used to say, 'Only those that can do should teach.'"

A good director or business leader is truly an inspiration. As cinematic acting coach David Lehman believes, "No one can teach you to be an actor. You are an actor or you are not. If you have the gift, it is also an obligation. All any good teacher can do is help you discover your unique creative soul in your work."

Ultimately, I believe that every leader's goal is to choose a team based on the members' skills and gifts, give the team members the tools they need to develop their gifts, and ultimately teach them, and then motivate them, to be the best they can be.

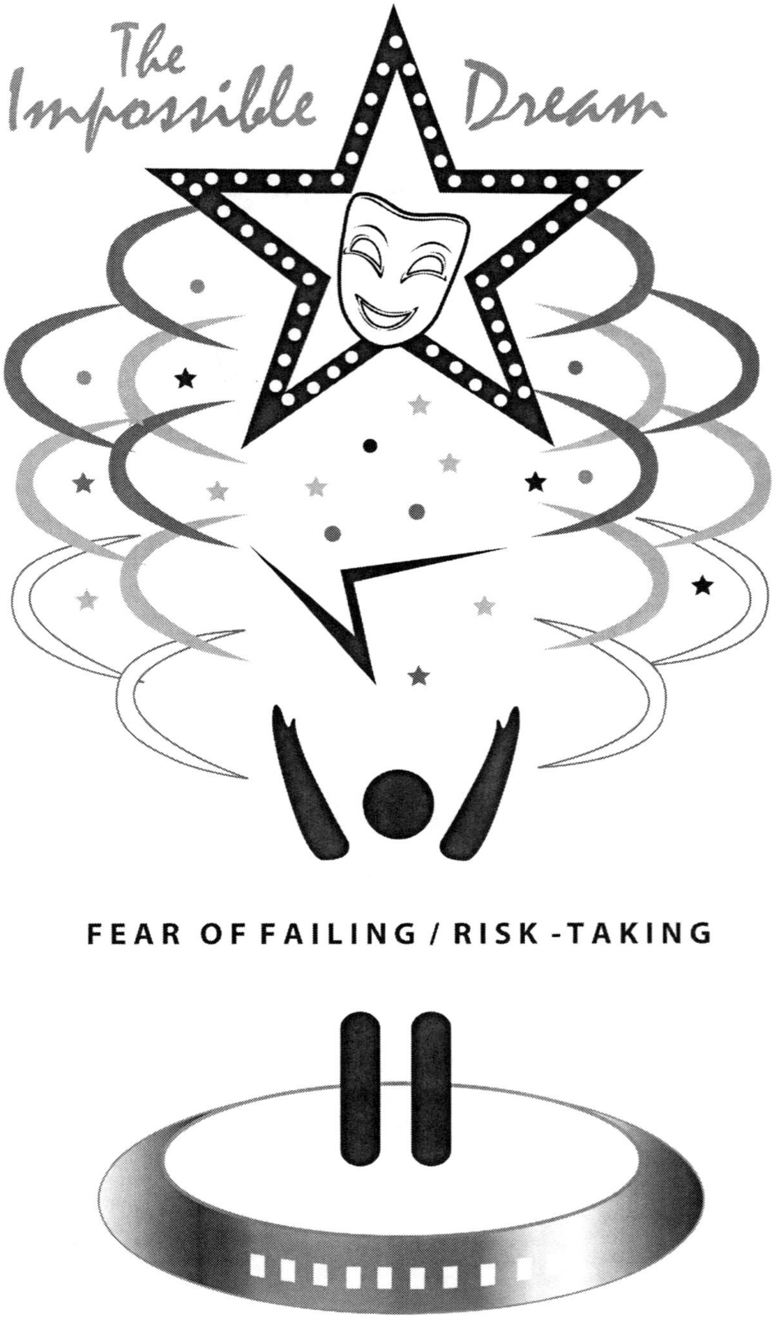

The Impossible Dream

FEAR OF FAILING / RISK-TAKING

Chapter 6

Still strove with his last ounce of courage To reach the unreachable star

Fear of Failing/Risk Taking

("The Impossible Dream" from *Man of La Mancha*
—Lyrics by Joe Darion)

Nothing is as scary or nerve-wracking to actors as an audition. Actors are putting themselves out to be judged as worthy to play a part, and the risk they take of being rejected is a very difficult one to swallow. Yet actors must do what they fear most or give up their craft. To be successful in business, and in life, each person must be willing to give up what she has in order to get what she wants. Without risk of failure, there can be no success.

So what about the paralyzing fear of failure known as stage fright? *Music Stand* quoted anonymously a wryly funny and true-to-life definition: "The unreasonable fear of performing for an audience that is only waiting to laugh at, jeer, and mutilate you for anything less than a perfect performance." Indeed, unknown to the general public, many famous actors are plagued with stage fright. How, then, do they overcome their fear and perform in spite of it?

Andrea Bocelli, a world-famous opera singer, commands millions of dollars for a concert and even more for an opera—yet he suffers from stage fright. When Barbara Walters asked him during a TV interview what he did to cure stage fright, he replied, "Nothing. I am afraid, and so I go on." What Andrea does is exactly what Humphrey Bogart preached: "The only thing you owe the public is a good performance." As they say, the show must go on—despite our fears of failure and rejection.

What is it that drives actors to take risk after risk and face failure over and over again on their paths to success? For me, it is the thrill of success, of setting a goal and meeting it, perhaps even surpassing it. The ride can be scary and risks must be taken, but in the end it is all worth it.

Every time I have faced the nightmare that is audition, I've faced a different but no less daunting challenge. When I had to sing a solo, for example, I was terrified. After the audition, I realized that it did not really matter whether I got the part; the part was secondary to the joy and pride I felt by having taken a risk to face my fear. Eventually, I found my real voice as an actor and began to audition for plays rather than musicals.

Since then, I've landed some wonderful roles in great plays. Yet even with my newfound success, each audition brings with it the intense fear of failing. Each time, I know that this time, no matter what has gone before, I could be rejected. But in all this, I have learned an important lesson that has served me well: I have learned to face rejection when it comes without taking it personally.

When a director is casting a show, he has a picture of the person he wants to cast for each role because he has a distinct perception of how he wants each role to be played. If you do not fit his picture, you will not be cast, no matter how objectively good you are.

I had a reminder of this at an audition for *Steel Magnolias*. I had played the show before and was confident that I was right for the role of at least one of the five interesting and unique women it features. At the audition, I read with another woman, and I thought I had done a great job. The director seemed very impressed with my performance and complimented me throughout my audition. Furthermore, after doing as many auditions as I have, I can pick up on how I am doing by the way the director acts, the things she says, and the questions she asks. After I finished my audition, I thought I had the part for sure. A few days later, I was elated when I got a call from the director, who had said she would only call the women who were cast.

The director told me that she felt she had to call to tell me how well I had done and how impressed she was with my acting skills. My heart started sinking: I could sense the "but" coming. She explained that she'd had thirteen very talented women audition, giving her a hard task to choose between them. In the end, she had chosen the five women who fit together best; it simply worked out that I was not one of them. She finished by requesting that I audition for another of her shows because she really wanted to work with me.

Even though I was disappointed, I was impressed that the director was kind enough to make the call. More often than not, the call never comes and the opportunity passes by. I have learned that not getting cast does not mean I did not do a good job: it just means I did not fit with what the director had in mind. If I thought every rejection was a reflection of my skills, I probably couldn't face the prospect of rejection again and would have given up on my passion long ago.

This doesn't mean that all you can do is shrug your shoulders and move on. I always ask for feedback when I don't get a part so that I can hone my skills and learn from my mistakes.

An acting magazine, *Backstage West*, had the following advice for actors working on a television or movie set: "Take nothing personally. Sometimes you will be asked to do something over and over, so don't begin to doubt your abilities. The director simply may not have time to tell you why—or that it is not you or your abilities, but simply time constraints, or comments from the writer. Do not take those actions or emotions personally. Stay flexible, adaptable, and professional, no matter what the circumstances." Good advice in all aspects of life.

I have mentioned before that my sons have also caught the acting bug. They learned this same lesson, and it has served them well in their business lives. For example, when Brian was about ten years old, he entered a talent competition; first prize was a contract with a management company. Brian was a wonderful singer, and he did a beautiful rendition of a popular song.

He was incredible—though you know you're hearing a mother talking. Brian didn't win, but he did come in second. First place went to a redheaded girl who tap-danced. The next day I received a call from the manager of the company offering the contract to the contest winner, asking to represent Brian. When I expressed surprise (because he had lost), she replied that redheaded children almost always win contests of this sort; she said companies like to use redheads in commercials. But she told me that Brian had talent and that she would like to send him on some auditions.

Brian and I traveled into New York City from New Jersey each time he was called for an audition. After his first audition, he waited by the phone for days and was disappointed when he did not get called back. I explained to him my philosophy about needing to fit into the profile for a particular job and told him that any lack of talent was not necessarily the reason he did not get the job. After a while he began to take rejections in stride.

Now, as a successful businessman and entrepreneur, he is not afraid of chasing his dreams and taking calculated risks in his attempts to get what he wants. He would tell you today that he learned how to see failure as a stepping stone—that if you do not try, you cannot win. Grant M. Bright, a trainer on leadership and teamwork says, "Failing many times does not make one a failure. Giving up makes one a failure."

I always encourage people I know to let their children become involved in theater, if for no other reason than that the work in theater teaches the lesson of handling rejection, overcoming it, and not letting it stop you from moving forward.

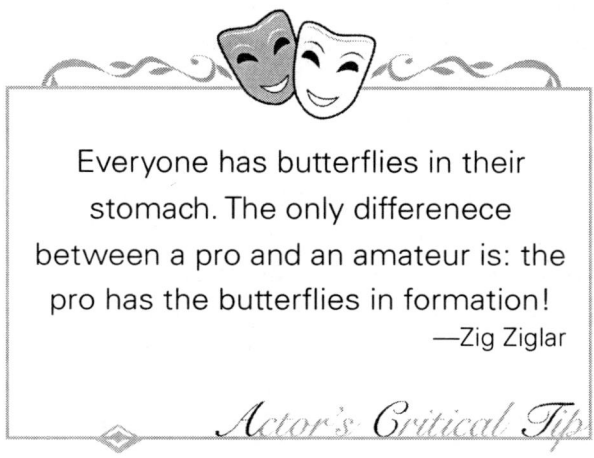

Everyone has butterflies in their stomach. The only differenece between a pro and an amateur is: the pro has the butterflies in formation!
—Zig Ziglar

Actor's Critical Tip

This attitude has served me well in business. One of my first careers was in sales. Talk about rejection! Once again, sales trainer Tom Hopkins: "For every yes, you first get four nos. Every time a prospect says 'No,' say, 'Thanks for the no,' knowing that after each 'no,' the 'yes' is getting closer." This concept puts rejection in a whole new light.

Brad Garrett, well-known for playing the bumbling brother of Ray Romano in *Everybody Loves Raymond*, said in an interview in August 2006, after the series had ended and he was looking for other work, "What really kept me going was [that] I was doing what I loved. I didn't always make a living at it, nor did I have people telling me I was good, but I knew that I had to do what I loved. It's being ready and prepared and knowing you are going to blow the majority of the auditions. It's a numbers game. You have to remember: it takes one person to say no and fifteen to say yes. People get bitter because you're so beaten by the time you get there." When asked what role or project he wanted to tackle next, he replied, "I'd love to go back to theater eventually. I'd love to do something dramatic in theater. Anything that scares me is important to do. And there's a lot that scares me. I'm 6'8", forty-six years old, and I have a night light. Although, that's not because I'm scared: I'm just addicted to shadow puppets."

When the late Paul Newman was asked what quality an actor needed most to succeed, he answered emphatically, "Tenaciousness!" This common thread in the world of the thespian can be seen and heard throughout the arts. Famous choreographer Debbie Allen, who is also a dancer, actor, producer, and director, told *Backstage Magazine* about the difficulties she had faced as an African American in Texas in the 1960s: "You know there are brick walls and glass ceilings and all that crap all over. That's why it's great that I am a dancer, because I'm used to the pain. Dancing gets you ready for the pain so you can take the pain and the criticism. 'No' for me means, 'Okay, not with you, but maybe somewhere else.' Keep trying somewhere else." She described her experience when she auditioned for the dance program at a liberal arts college, recalling, "I was the best thing at the audition. Then when it was over, I said, 'Well, when do I start?' And the man said, 'Well—I am sorry, but you should go into something different. Your body is not right for dance.' That was terrible: it was hard."

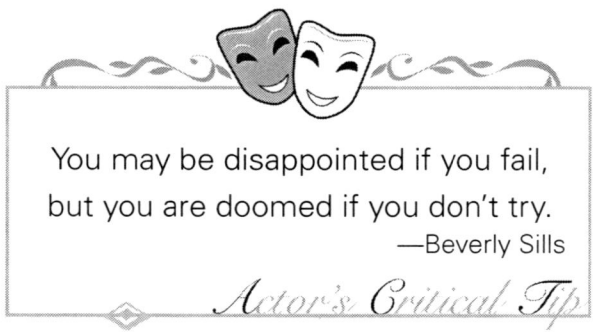

You may be disappointed if you fail, but you are doomed if you don't try.
—Beverly Sills

Actor's Critical Tip

Though she considers the experience one of the most painful of her early life, Allen also sees it as a turning point. In the next four decades, Allen won three Emmy Awards, two Tony nominations, and a Golden

Globe. To her students at her dance academy, her advice now is, "You must not know fear. Fear is someone you must not know, and you must try everything. Try different things and things you are not used to. Try something different."

In business, as in life, fear of failing is the obstacle to reaching goals. An aspiring actor must learn how to conquer his fear, or how to function in the presence of it, and must be able to embrace risk—to get out there and go for it.

This principle has many applications in the business world. Ask yourself: are you willing to take risks, to try something different? Eleanor Roosevelt said it best: "Remember, no one can make you feel inferior without your permission."

The lessons you learn in the acting profession can be valuable. Nowhere is there a profession that contains as much failure and rejection as acting. Only a tiny percentage of hopefuls succeed. And, counter intuitively, sometimes talent has nothing to do with it; success is simply being in the right place at the right time. The phenomenon of shows like *American Idol, Dancing with the Stars, America's Got Talent*, and *So You Think You Can Dance* substantiates this. Nearly all of the contestants featured on these shows would have remained forever in obscurity had they not been given the opportunity to audition. Just the opportunity of appearing— even only to suffer a loss—is an invaluable chance that most never get.

Take Jennifer Hudson, who made it to the top ten on *American Idol* only to be voted off the show. Unfazed, she landed a role in *Dreamgirls* for which she won an Oscar. When interviewed on a TV talk show, she said, "I just didn't get the votes. It wasn't meant to be. Things happen for a reason, even if you can't see that right away. If I hadn't been eliminated from *American Idol*, I wouldn't be starring in *Dreamgirls* now."

Actors are constantly being rejected, refused, and ignored. Many persist and persevere, waiting tables or bartending just to pay the bills so they can continue to chase their dream. I believe that if there was anything that brought actors the joy and happiness that acting does, they would have done it long ago. But it is the passion and the drive to do what they love that frees their souls and keeps them keeping on.

Does your profession feed your soul? If not, go back and read chapter two again. If possible, find your passion in your work, and if that is impossible, then fill your life with your passion as an avocation. Happiness comes from following your passion. Do what you are passionate about.

Whether you are doing what you love or just doing what you have to do to stay afloat, you will ultimately face failure, fear, and rejection. When you do what you fear most, you conquer your fear. In every walk of life, you will experience times of immense fear, but in those times you must trust in yourself and your abilities and know that you can do it—whatever it is. Have trust in what you know and who you are, and that will give you the power you need to go forward. Perhaps you will succeed and perhaps you won't, but at least you will be moving forward, closer to your potential.

Famous actor Alan Arkin, nominated for several Oscars, including one for his role as the grandfather in the wonderful movie *Little Miss Sunshine*, spoke in a *Backstage Magazine* interview about the scene in the movie when Grandpa reminds his son Richard, who has failed yet again at a business venture, that losers are people who never try at all. Ultimately, he tells Richard that he is proud of him. In the article, Arkin also talks about working with the comedy ensemble Second City. He said he loved the company, in part, because it was a place where it was okay to fail. "Nobody lets you make mistakes anywhere anymore. Making a mistake is a crucial learning experience, and knowing you can fall on your face and find out where you could go and where you can't go was really, really important."

What atmosphere surrounds failure and risk at your place of business? Are you a manager who encourages risk taking? Consider what happens to you when you fail. Do you think, "Oh, no—I've messed up big time, and now *everyone* is going to think I am a failure"? Do you use your experiences of failure to grow and move forward, or do you retreat instead?

Ultimately, what is important is not the mistake you made or the failure you think you are, but how you handle it and how everyone else affected by it handles it. Rocco Scanza, director of Cornell University's conflict resolution program, stated in a newspaper interview, "Timing is critical. The sooner the problem is addressed, the more likely [that] a workable solution can be achieved." More to the point: mistakes happen, but the real question is whether you are taking responsibility for your mistakes and learning from them or are instead blaming others for them. Scanza says, "Many employees do not own up to their mistakes, because they fear retaliation or—worse—being fired. So it is up to the managers to create an atmosphere in which coming clean does not necessarily mean employees will find themselves mailing out résumés the next day."

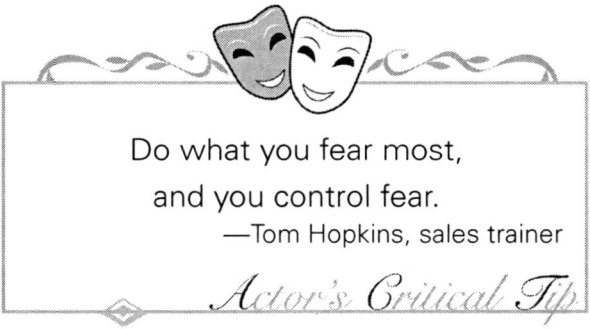

Do what you fear most,
and you control fear.
—Tom Hopkins, sales trainer

Actor's Critical Tip

In 2002, I attended a business seminar in which Keith Harrell, who calls himself Mr. Enthusiasm, spoke to the group about being enthusiastic and having a positive attitude. But what resonated most with me was the following statement: "Worry is a waste, because 40 percent of what we worry about already happened, 30 percent never happens, and 30 percent happens despite our worry."

Easier said than done. So how do we do what needs to be done even when we are afraid? I believe that seeing is believing, but more important is remembering that believing is seeing and seeing is doing. Change what you believe and you can change what you do. Clear as mud? Ask yourself the following question: What would I do in this situation if I were not afraid to do it? Then, with a grain of common sense, do it!

James Dyson, an industrial designer of vacuum cleaners, said it so well that Starbucks put his quote on their coffee cup holders. "The Way I See It #157," quoting James, says, "Some of the best inventive moments were born out of 'wrong thinking.' Most people start out going the right way, or in nearly the right direction—and so all follow the same path. But the wrong way will lead to mistakes that help you learn, and that can provoke you to new discoveries and ideas—the kind of original ideas that come to life when we dare to be different, keep an open mind, and have no fear of failure."

Do you have the courage and confidence to let yourself indulge in "wrong thinking"? Will you take the chance of making a mistake and failing? Do you have the courage to take risks and be vulnerable? The courage paradox states that we must be fully committed and yet also aware that we might be completely wrong.

And this is what courage is: the strength of will to go all in for what we believe instead of hanging back, paralyzed with fears borne out of what-ifs. In every situation, remember that sometimes you make the right decision, and sometimes you make the decision right. Do your due diligence and make the decision based on the information you have at the time. Then trust in yourself and make it work. If you make a mistake, go back and fix it. Most decisions are not life and death and can be remedied if needed. Do not remain frozen. Take the risk.

Stanford University professor Robert Sutton, author of *Weird Ideas That Work*, points out that Albert Einstein and Pablo Picasso failed frequently but were willing to risk failure in order to succeed—and succeed they did. You must do the things that scare you, must take on the big assignments at work, must give the speech to a large audience, must try an experiment, must let yourself be uncomfortable, must speak up with conviction and confidence—and you must do it all regardless of how scared you are.

I recommend Marlo Thomas's book *The Right Words at the Right Time*, which reminds us of the strength we can find amid life's challenges when we take the right perspective, no matter how unfamiliar or how outside our experience it may be. Some of Thomas's words came from people just like you and me. For example, a taxi driver related to Thomas that his uncle used to say, "Don't be scared of the side streets and back roads—they might get you there quicker." Or take Thomas' friend who told his first boss, "If you keep doing things the same way, you'll never get different results." Similarly, a daughter of one of her friends was nervous about her chances of running for class president. Her teacher said, "If you run, you might not win. But if you don't run, you certainly won't win."

Think about the big risks you have taken in your life. Even if you failed, weren't you glad you took the risk and tried? I've often heard it said that we tend to regret most the things we did not do. Doing, even when it leads to failure, is no cause for regret. After all, we all experience failure and disappointment in our lives. Sometimes disappointments turn out for the best, causing us to change course. Regret, on the other hand, is about something we didn't do; disappointment is simply about something we didn't achieve. We always wonder how things might have turned out had we gone ahead and tried. The regret we feel is wholly different from disappointment, which, although it may hurt, can be analyzed as we can ask ourselves why we got the result we did and how we can prevent it from happening again.

When we avoid regret by risking disappointment, it's a certainty that we'll be disappointed more often. And that's okay. Just keep your expectations reasonable and realistic, don't expect too much out of a sense of entitlement, and always have a contingency plan.

For example, while I wrote this book, I auditioned for a couple of shows but did not get cast. Each time I lost a part, I told myself that I would use the time I would have spent in rehearsal to work on my book instead. I decided that that was what I was supposed to do at this time in my life. I believe that everything happens for a reason and that people ultimately end up where they are supposed to be. And when we do, we grow through our disappointments and challenges to become better—and more capable—people. "It's no use sitting upon me," said Winston Churchill, "for I am India rubber and I bounce!" So should you also. Dr. Joyce Brothers advised, long ago in a TV interview, that you take care of yourself, go easy on yourself, take inventory of the good things in your life, enjoy each day, understand that disappointment can help reinvent your life, laugh, and tap into the India rubber inside of you.

Sales trainer Tom Hopkins, in his book *How to Master the Art of Selling*, tells us, "I am not judged by the number of times I fail, but by the number of times I succeed: and the number of times I succeed is in direct proportion to the number of times I fail and keep trying."

Before I share tips and tools for applying some of the principles we've discussed in this chapter, I'd like to leave you with some famous quotes on this subject that say things better than I ever could:

"When one door closes, another door opens." Helen Keller

"If you risk NOTHING, then you risk EVERYTHING." Geena Davis

"The first and greatest commandment is *don't let them scare you.*" Elmer Davis

"Courage is very important. Like a muscle, it's strengthened by use." Ruth Gordon

"I go with what scares me." Helen Hunt, on choosing roles

"Until you try, you do not know what you cannot do." Henry James

"Do the things you fear to do, and the death of fear is sure." Dale Carnegie

"Don't cry because it is over; smile because it happened." Anonymous

"A king once asked his wise men, 'Give me a statement that can be used in any situation,' and the statement was 'This too shall pass.'" Abraham Lincoln

"Fall seven times, stand up eight." Anonymous

"One of the secrets of life is to make stepping stones out of stumbling blocks." Jack Penn

"Finish each day and be done with it. You have done what you could; some blunders and absurdities have crept in; forget them as soon as you can. Tomorrow is a new day; you shall begin it serenely and with too high a spirit to be encumbered with your old nonsense." Ralph Waldo Emerson

TIPS AND TOOLS

Study the failures/mistakes

To understand success, study failure and understand it.

The 3A approach to recovery: recovery and resolution

It is imperative that you have a recovery and resolution process when communication fails or when a mistake is made because of a lack of good communication. The 3A approach is to acknowledge, apologize, and action.

Acknowledge

If you acknowledge that a mistake was made or that communication failed, you demonstrate that you received the other person's communication and that you understand why she is upset or angry. This begins to defuse her anger because she knows that you heard her when she was complaining. Actively listen, then repeat back what you hear.

Apologize

Even if you are not the one at fault, apologize for causing stress to the other person. Often people are hesitant to apologize because they believe that doing so implies that they were wrong or made a mistake. Either people are hesitant to admit to mistakes or they simply do not believe that they were at fault. Either way, apologize. You need not blame yourself. Simply say that you are sorry that the incident happened and that you are sorry that the other person feels bad or is upset. A simple apology can defuse another person's anger immediately.

Action

Do something to make things right. This is the most important step to recovering from a mistake, whether yours or someone else's. Without this step, the other two steps will not resolve anything—they may in fact make the situation worse. Too often when someone makes a mistake, he apologizes but then continues on to explain why the situation happened, and even goes so far as to explain why it was not really his fault or his company's fault. In such a situation, the injured party rightly becomes even angrier. People in these situations don't want rationalization—they want action. They want to know what you are going to do about the problem: how you will fix it or make it right. It is important to agree upon some action that the offended party can accept. Taking the right action can cement a relationship, sometimes making it even better than it was before the mishap occurred.

Here is one example: "Mr. (Customer Name), it is obvious that something has gone wrong (or our communication has failed). I apologize for any inconvenience or stress this has caused you. Let's discuss what we can do to remedy the situation for you."

I once worked with an automotive dealer who was trying to improve his dealership's process for fixing cars right the first time. Many of his technicians were young and inexperienced. One day, a tech mistakenly left a rag on top of a customer's engine block. As the customer drove away, the engine got hot, the rag got dragged inside the engine, and a fire started in the customer's car. The customer called the shop, and the manager immediately sent a tow truck and driver to bring the woman back to the shop. The woman's car was in bad shape. The manager knew he was facing a possible lawsuit—especially since the customer was a lawyer. Upon the customer's return to the shop, the manager took complete responsibility for the tech's error and apologized profusely to the customer. The manager assured the woman that he would take care of all of the repairs, and he offered her a loaner car for as long as it took to repair her vehicle.

Now, any good manager would have done that—and most would have stopped there. But this manager then sent a huge bouquet of flowers to the customer's house that evening, along with a gift certificate to a very expensive restaurant in town. The customer was so impressed with his resolution of the matter that she told all of her friends to go to his shop for service, saying that although everyone makes mistakes, not many people admit to it and then go above and beyond to make matters right for the affected customer.

Another great example happened at a five-star restaurant. On a crowded Saturday night, a group of eight showed up claiming they had a reservation. When the reservation book was checked, the staff discovered that the reservation had been made for Sunday night. The group admitted that the mistake could have been theirs, but they asked to be seated nevertheless, if possible. Because no tables were available, the owner stepped in, ordered a limousine for the eight guests, and had them taken to an excellent restaurant nearby. And as if that were not enough, imagine the group's surprise when the owner showed up at their table and asked whether the service and the food were exceeding their expectations. The group assured him that they were very happy with what he had done for them. To put the cherry on top, when they asked for the check, they were told that the check had been taken care of. Can you imagine the number of times each person in that group told that story? It is impossible to buy that kind of advertising.

Use the ready, SET, go approach

I can't take credit for this one. I read it somewhere, unaccredited. I'll say a big thank you to whoever developed the concept. This approach, the ready, SET, go approach, will generate a positive frame of mind that is future–oriented.

When bad things happen to you:

See them as temporary. Will this be a big deal ten years from now? Externalize. Step back and see the big picture. Don't take things personally.
Take action. Make or plan a formula for correcting the issue if possible. Focus on the things you can control.

Whenever you fail, remember the following:

The greatest quarterbacks complete only six of ten passes.
The best basketball players make only 50 percent of their shots.
The top oil companies, with all their geologists, drill ten dry holes for every one wet one.
And even the most successful actors flunk twenty-nine auditions for a television commercial before they land one.

-Council Fire Letter
Published by the Boy Scouts of America

The Interview

I HOPE I GET IT- I NEED THIS JOB

Chapter 7

I need this job,
Oh God I need this show

The Interview

("I Hope I Get It" from *A Chorus Line*
—Lyrics by Edward Kleban)

The stage is set.
The audience is in their seats.
The actor is in costume backstage.
The music is cued.

The actor enters wearing a business suit and a marching band leader's hat. The music for *Strike Up the Band* is playing. The actor takes center stage and delivers a monologue about the role of the band leader. He also asks and answers such questions as:

What is the role of the band leader?
What people make up the band?
What instruments do the band members play?
Who chooses the instruments and music used by the band?
How are the band members taught to play?
How does the leader motivate the members to march together and
    follow him?

Does this sound like you are at a show or performance on stage? No, this is an actual job interview. As a matter of fact, it was one of my first high-level job interviews. The ad said LOOKING FOR THE WORLD'S BEST SALES TRAINER. And guess what? I got the job, beating out three other highly qualified candidates. These candidates, by the way, probably had more experience and expertise than I had at the time. I had done some sales training, but I had no real product experience in the industry for which I was interviewing. I knew I had to get my act together—to dazzle my audience. I was confident in my ability to sell and to train others to sell, even though I was not a subject matter expert in the product. I knew I needed to keep the attention of my audience on my skills and abilities as a sales trainer, rather than on my lack of product knowledge, and I knew I could learn quickly.

I decided to compare a sales trainer to a marching band director and to talk about how the director trains the band to play the instruments much as a sales trainer trains the salespeople to sell their product. The band director teaches the band how to march together in unison to create just the right look, in alignment with each other.

The sales trainer motivates each novice salesperson to create an environment in which customers want to invest in the product or service. The band leader motivates the band members and requires long hours of practice from them. And the effective sales trainer shows how using a script and practicing it until the salesperson owns it makes for effective, persuasive selling. Product knowledge, like knowing a piece of music, is essential for a good performance.

Both the band director and the sales trainer must be adept at developing a team that is aligned with the common goal and whose members are ready and able to work together and support each other in attaining it. Both have to train their respective students to wow the audience, to make the music, to create an environment in which the audience buys what the individual or team is selling. The salesperson must leave the audience applauding, giving rave reviews, and asking for encore performances.

In another job interview, I performed a magic trick. And I got that job, too. In both cases, being able to use my acting skills to paint a picture for the managers who were conducting the interview gave me an edge over my competition.

These interviews took place after I'd had the opportunity to practice and hone my skills during some interesting auditions. For example, I remember my first. My son Brian had been invited to audition for a show. An invitation is a pretty good sign that someone is interested in you, and your probability of being cast is high. I was in the habit of accompanying Brian when he was cast and to rehearsals; he was only nine years old at the time. After his first show, I asked to be put to work, and so I learned how to operate the spotlight and then the lighting board. Nowadays, computers are used to control stage lighting, but in those days, everything was done by hand.

This time, I decided to audition for the show myself because I saw they were using a women's chorus. The show was *Joseph and the Amazing Technicolor Dreamcoat*. I was a wreck because I had to sing alone for the audition. Although I love to sing, I have a voice that is okay for a chorus but not for a lead role. Singing alone is scary for me. I got through it—barely. I wasn't very good, but I think the director felt sorry for me and cast me anyway. Acting and singing in the show was an amazing, wonderful experience and one I will always cherish.

For my next audition, I again had to sing. This time I did not know the director, my son was not already cast, and the audition was open, so everyone who was auditioning got to watch everyone else audition. I was a wreck, and when my turn came I opened my mouth to sing and nothing—I mean absolutely *nothing*—came out. I was mortified. But the judges gave me another chance, and I squeaked through to get a part in the chorus. After a few more chorus parts in musicals, I realized that if I was going to get bigger and better parts, I would be better off auditioning for nonmusicals. And when I did, the auditioning process became fun, and my fear disappeared—because I was now working from my strength.

When you leverage your strengths, you can take risks with more confidence. As I continued to audition and got cast in significant leading roles, my interviewing skills also improved. I began to use what I had learned during the audition process to assist me in my job interviews, such as the ones I described at the beginning of this chapter.

The goal of an interview: getting "cast" in the job of your choice.

Actor's Critical Tip

Auditioning for a part is very similar to interviewing for a job. Both can be stressful, even terrifying. But there is a tremendous crossover of skills that we can apply.

During the audition process, actors must sell themselves to the director and the members of the production crew. In a job interview, interviewees must also sell themselves in much the same way to earn the position.

TIPS AND TOOLS

Interviewee Techniques

The techniques the successful actor often uses in an audition can be applied to any job interview.

- Research the industry in which you are interested. Know as much as you can about its products and services.

- Research the product or service provided by the company with whom you are interviewing.

- Engage and entertain your audience—the people conducting the interview.

- Creatively demonstrate your skills and talents.

- Prepare your script in advance.

- Memorize your script so well that the words become second nature.

- Be ready to describe who you are, what you have accomplished in the past, and why you are the right person for the job.

- Include industry buzzwords—and know what they mean.

- Develop a list of questions to ask:

  - What is the role and what responsibilities come with the job?

  - What are the expectations and desired outcomes in the position?

  - What are the working hours?

  - What is the vacation policy?

  - What benefits are included?

  - What is the salary? What are the perks?

  - What advancement opportunities does the position offer?

  - To whom will you report?

  - Who will report to you?

- Use body language to sell yourself. We'll talk more about this in chapter eight, when we discuss presentation.

- Practice, practice, practice (rehearse) your performance.

- Be confident and prepared to wow your audience by focusing on what you bring to the position.

- Engage all the senses of your audience whenever possible.

- Dress for the part. Be sure your appearance reflects the image you are trying to convey without being distracting. Marilyn Henry, writing for *Backstage Magazine*, says,
  The color you choose to wear to an interview or an audition can have a psychological impact on the casting director or interviewer. Red is associated with passion, ambition, desire, and assertiveness. Green has a calming, balanced,

nonthreatening energy and is restful to the eye. Deeper shades like forest, cucumber, avocado and emerald are effective for meetings. Blue can make you appear credible and confident. Purple is associated with creativity. Avoid yellow, orange, hot pink, and very bright colors, as they can cause anxiety and hyperactivity.

Grey represents passivity and no commitment. Browns are best worn as slacks and skirts. Blacks are a favorite, and reveal that you are disciplined, strong-willed, independent, and opinionated. Black can also create distance, making one appear aloof, dramatic, mysterious, and unapproachable. Black is worn best from the waist down, and not next to the face. Try on your clothing in natural light."

- Use props effectively.

- Be confident about your being the best person for the job. Talk about your past successes. Describe how previous companies or individuals benefited from having you as an employee.

- Take a deep breath to reduce your stage fright. Refocus, and then continue. Thorough preparation will help you minimize your anxiety.

- Close, and wait for the applause. Finish well and then ask when the decision will be made as well as how you will be contacted.

- Ask if you may call back in a day or two. This shows that you are genuinely interested and that you are willing to take the responsibility to call. Do not be intrusive, however, by placing many calls. Try to reach the interviewer a couple of times, and leave a sincere, friendly message asking for a call back, whether or not you got the position. Casting director Mali Finn gives this advice to actors: "The one thing I learned when I came to LA is that you never leave a meeting without another meeting. This is your business. You're your own boss. You need to be the CEO of your own company, and you need to network."

- Send a thank-you note immediately after the interview. This indicates that you are professional and thoughtful.

- If you end up not being offered the job, thank the interviewer and ask if she can share with you the reasons you were not selected so that you can improve your skills and performance in the future.

Ana Gasteyer of *Saturday Night Live* fame boasts, "I actually like auditioning. It gives you the slight illusion that you're auditioning them, as well, and it affords you insight about the part and the people you will be working with."

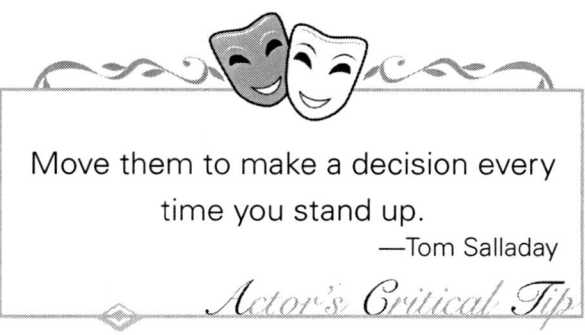

Move them to make a decision every
time you stand up.
—Tom Salladay
Actor's Critical Tip

Advice from talent agents mirrors the advice of career counselors. Paulo Andres from the Link Talent Group in Valley Village, California, says, "Your mindset must be in place in regard to the audition. Like any other job interview that you have been in, it is you on your best day applying for a job. There should never be an attempt to experiment with the craft and 'practice' something at the audition. The scene must be your best work on this day. Common basics include plenty of rest the night before, arriving a half hour early, and, before getting out of the car, leaving all your life's problems in the vehicle." Tom Ingegno from Omnipop Talent Group of New York and California advises, "It is always important to leave a little something behind at every audition—like a good impression." Michael Katz, who owns a New York management company, suggests starting with the 3 R's. The first one is "research," the second "rehearse," and the third "relax."

Bring your passion, your energy, and your enthusiasm into the interview. It is important that you be persuasive in order to sell yourself. When you demonstrate passion and excitement about a position or product, it is contagious. Gregory D. Hayes, the executive director of the career services center at the University of Dayton, says, "Show your passion by talking about your experience, education, and skills with a clear love of what you do and what you want to do. Passion shows your love of the business you're in. It's a means of convincing the job interviewer [that] this is the job you really want to do—and that you can do it. I got all of my jobs because of my passion for what I do. I prepared thoroughly, researched each company, and articulated my skills in a convincing and positive way. I urge my students to state exactly why they want the job and to say it with passion." It's interesting how career counselors and acting coaches give similar advice!

James F. Fitzgerald, chairman of the board of Career Transitions Center of Chicago, says, "Enthusiasm for the work and excitement for the challenge and the opportunity to solve any problems the potential employer has— that makes you stand out from other people who have the same skills." He suggests that to prepare for the interview, you should talk to yourself in advance and say, "I love this business. Employers want to hire people who feel as passionate as they do about the work. The real challenge is to be enthusiastic without sounding desperate."

Have fun and enjoy the process. Every audition and every interview has its own story and set of experiences. If you are open to learning, you will enhance your skills and improve with practice. Learn to overcome your nervousness—or at least to hide it and "fake it till you make it."

Michael Kostroff writes a column for *Backstage Magazine* called "Talk Back." I enjoyed his take on nerves in an article titled "The Power of Voodoo": "No one hires nervous actors. Would you hire a trembling, glassy-eyed babysitter, or a stammering perspiring surgeon?" Kostroff goes on to teach some psychological tricks in another article, *Audition Voodoo*: "Never go to an audition to get a job. Instead, go to help solve a casting problem. Remember that this is just one audition. 'It isn't the top of the mountain; it's just a step on the way.'" Here is one exercise he shares: "Consider that near the interview or audition there is a hospital where someone is dying and someone is being born. All around you, huge, important events are happening. Suddenly your audition isn't quite as big or scary."

Or, to put it more forcefully, Gower Champion sent his cast this telegram on opening nights: "Just remember, two billion Chinamen don't give a @#*% about what happens tonight!" Regardless of whether you get the job, auditions give you the opportunity to do what you love for a few minutes.

Interviewer techniques

If a company or business is to grow, it is crucial that the right people be hired. The person who is conducting the interview needs to exercise skills to properly identify those people who have the knowledge, skills, talents, and personal skills and strengths to get the job done well. Here are some good questions to ask:

1. What are some of your best qualities? This question helps to assess self-esteem. It is important to be able to express the good qualities. Being uncomfortable talking about these qualities should be a red flag.

2. What are some of your greatest accomplishments? This is something any good candidate should be prepared to discuss.

3. As a manager, how would you recognize an employee? This can also be asked as to how one would recognize a coworker.

4. What is your process for decision making?

Del J. Still, the president of Marketing Development Systems in California, says, "Some 95 percent of all interviewers make a decision whether to hire or not within the first minutes of the interview. The time remaining is just self-fulfilling prophecy as the interviewer gathers information to justify the decision."

In looking at the crossover of skills and situations between interviewing and auditioning, let's focus on some quotes from business people and authorities on acting. In *Backstage West*, a magazine for actors, Sarah Kuhn writes an article called "Ask a Director." The question she poses is, "What quality do you value most in auditions?" Ben Bradley, the resident director at the Fountain Theater in Los Angeles, says, "When actors come to audition for me, I expect first that they come in prepared. My assessment of the actor starts when they walk in the room."

The writer–director of the independent film *Adam and Steve* Reports that he looks for courage: "I cast people that show up that were completely committed to the film and it was almost as if they already had the job. You want to work with people who are excited and enthusiastic. That's what you want: someone to bring something of themselves, something original."

Alternatively, "The first quality I look for in an audition is sanity," says John Clancy, the artistic director of the New York International Film Festival. "When a human being walks in comfortable in their own skin, breathing normally, it's like water in the desert." Rob Marshall, the director of *Memoirs of a Geisha* and *Chicago*, states, interestingly, "You know what's interesting? Good directors, most directors, want you to come in and be good and succeed. They're not looking to see what's wrong with you; they're looking to see what's right with you. I look for somebody who is passionate about what they do and [who] lets themselves come out. They don't try to be something, because they're enough. That's what I want to say: You're plenty. You're interesting enough. Let me see that person. Whether you are right or wrong for the role, that won't matter; I'll be impressed by what you bring to it."

Shaggy Dog and *Varsity Blues* director, Brian Robbins, sums it up by saying, "I am always appreciative when someone comes in, and they are extremely focused, and they've really thought about it and are prepared.

If they have questions, they're the right questions, and they're really focused on killing it."

And there's some good advice from these directors that can apply to anyone who is in a position of the interviewer or the interviewee: be prepared, be committed, be confident, be excited, be enthusiastic, ask good questions, have fun, and go after what you want.

Razzle Dazzle Them

Show

PRESENTATION SKILLS

Chapter 8

Give 'em an act that's unassailable, They'll wait a year 'till you're available

Presentation Skills

(*"Razzle Dazzle"* from *Chicago* —Lyrics by Roger Mason)

Anyone who has put on a good presentation for two or more people is already an actor and just doesn't know it. The skills actors use on stage are directly related to presentation skills in general. For one thing, the ability to capture an audience in the first few minutes is crucial. Stage presence is very powerful and a necessity if the audience is to enjoy a show. If the goal of the presenter is for the audience to learn something, the presenter must have strong stand-up presentation skills. In this chapter, I make the connection between the actor, who has the talent to engage and entertain, and the trainer, presenter, salesperson or anyone in business who needs to do the same thing.

The ultimate presentation is live theater. Every day, movie and television actors show up on theatrical stages across the country to perform in front of a live audience. They do this because there's nothing like the feeling of interacting with the energy of a live audience. It is also very scary in that there are no do-overs or retakes. The performance must be tight and perfect the first time. So how does the actor get it right performance after performance? And what about mistakes? When they happen, how does the actor handle a forgotten line, an incorrect cue from a scene partner, or a technical error with the sound or the set?

After many years in the chorus, I played Edith in a wonderful show titled *Never Too Late*. It was my first leading role, in a small community theater group from a local church. The town was very supportive—the performance sold out.

All but one of the cast members had some theater experience. The one who did not was an older gentleman from the community who played the part of the town's mayor. He appeared in two scenes, with about five to ten lines in each. During rehearsals, he did an excellent job, and he seemed to know his lines well. None of us in the cast were prepared for what happened opening night—when the poor guy was struck with a major case of stage fright. It was the first scene of the play, and about five of us were on stage, discussing an upcoming event in the town. I gave the mayor his cue line ... but no response from the mayor was forthcoming. He looked at me and paused, and I saw that deer-in-the-headlights expression that every actor fears.

It is the look that says *I forgot my lines*. The look was not enough for the mayor; he looked at me and muttered under his breath, through clenched teeth, "I forgot my line." A woman in the third row repeated it: "He forgot his line." We could all hear the ripples of laughter filter through the first couple of rows. We did what more experienced actors do; we nonchalantly started feeding him questions in an effort to jump-start his memory. He eventually said something close to what his line had been, and the scene continued.

But the mayor was not done yet. Later, in Act 2, the fear struck him again, and again he froze. He did remember that his last line of the scene before he was to exit was, "I'll say no more." When, in the middle of the scene, he forgot the rest of his lines, he looked out to the audience, then to his scene partner, and proclaimed, "I'll say no more." And off he went, leaving the other actor open-mouthed and alone on the stage. We had to add some lines into the next scene so that the audience could get the info that was vital to the show.

Perhaps this is an extreme example, but it's not an isolated one. Mistakes and accidents do happen, and actors must be prepared to cover them up so that the audience thinks it's all just a part of the show.

Remember the story I told earlier about when the music that was cued to play never started? The cast and crew laughed about both incidents later, but at the time, things were pretty scary on the stage. The important thing was making sure that the audience had no idea that mistakes had been made—that they did not see or sense the sinking feeling in the pit of our stomachs.

Every actor remembers the bloopers: phones don't ring, music doesn't play, things fall down on the set, someone drops something, someone else trips—the bloopers go on and on and on. Mistakes are inevitable, but with no do-overs allowed, the professional actor stays in character and makes every scene work for the audience.

Every reader, at some point in her life—some more than others—will be in the spotlight and expected to perform, whether before a boss, a colleague, a friend, or a significant other. The presentation may be only to one person or it may be to a small group or even a large audience. In every case, consider it live theater: you, on the stage of life.

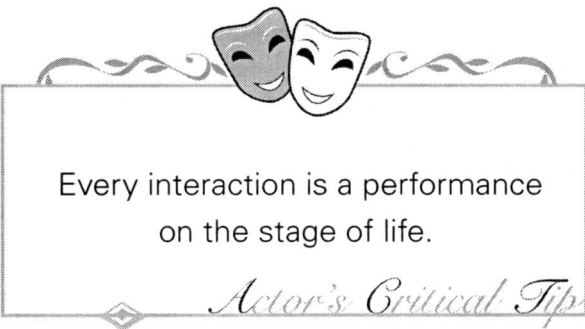

Every interaction is a performance
on the stage of life.

Actor's Critical Tip

Your performance will be watched and judged. Will it earn applause? Will it get a standing ovation? Will the audience request an encore? That's all up to you. You can use all these techniques in business and your personal life if you approach each presentation like an actor approaches every performance. Learn how to prepare, how to handle and recover from mistakes, how to use body language to communicate, how to read the feedback you are getting from your audience, and how to relax and have fun, knowing in your heart that you will be deserving of the applause you receive for your role in the show.

Let's take some time discussing some easy techniques you can use to perfect your performance.

Planning and preparation

Although when an actor or presenter speaks he seems as if he is speaking normally and naturally to his audience, very few presenters can just wing this easy manner and present their material well. To be comfortable with your material, you must know your topic and be confident that you can present it well. Know why you are speaking and to whom are you speaking. You might be speaking to persuade, to inform, to teach, to motivate, to entertain, to present, to accept something, or for any of many other reasons. Knowing to whom you are speaking is very important. Who is your audience? Does your audience know something about your topic, or do its members have no clue? Does your audience want to be there, or were the members of your audience forced to attend? Is your audience paying to see or hear your presentation? What do the members of your audience have in common with each other and with you? Answering these questions will help you prepare your presentation to meet the needs of your audience, so do your research ahead of time—it pays off.

Prepare what you want to say. Does your presentation's content meet the needs of your audience? Should buzzwords be used? Should questions be asked? Your presentation might include facts and figures or quotes from well-known people. Also, telling a story is usually well received. Remember to give examples; consider using props. Some presenters like to start with a joke—but make sure it is appropriate for your audience.

I start many of my presentations with something from Tony Jeary's book *Inspire Any Audience*. He suggests that you start your presentation by telling the group that participants typically fall into four basic categories, or mental states. The first audience type is the Prisoner. This person does not want to be there. He would rather be anywhere than listening to another talk. Someone else made the decision for him: he had no choice about whether to attend but was told to "Show up!" Some in the audience always snicker at this; I point out that they are probably my prisoners. I tell them that I welcome all prisoners and that although a prisoner is not there by choice, they do have a choice about what they take out of the presentation. So I ask them to take something away, to be rehabilitated, maybe even to learn something.

The second type is the Vacationer. This is the employee who will volunteer to attend any presentation as long as it gets her out of work. Usually more laughs are forthcoming. Vacationers are usually willing to raise hands and admit to this role. The vacationer is happy to be there, but for the wrong reasons. I ask the vacationer to have fun and to take away a souvenir of her vacation in the form of some new piece of information she did not know before.

The third type is the Graduate. This is the person who thinks he doesn't need to be there; he believes he already knows everything there is to know about the subject and doesn't expect to learn anything new. I admit that this is the hardest audience type to engage. I simply ask graduates to be willing to share their wisdom, knowledge, and experience with the rest of us.

The last type is my favorite—the Student. This person is always eager to learn something new, no matter how old she is or how educated she might be. The student is an attentive, hardworking participant who wants to hear what you've come to say.

After explaining the types of audience members, I tell them what I hope they will get from my presentation and ask everyone in the audience to find the student within.

I share my personal mission statement and assure them that if they will be present with me for the duration, they will leave with at least one new thing that will enhance the quality of their lives and help them to be more effective personally and professionally. Indeed, that's my goal when I perform or speak before an individual or a group: to leave my audience better than I found it.

All presentations should have a beginning, middle, and an end. Some say it this way: *Tell them what you're going to be telling them, then tell them, and then tell them what it was that you told them.* Start with the purpose or goal of your speech; tell your audience why you, and they, are there. Then give them the meat of what you have to tell them. Lay it all out—give it your best shot. Then, as you finish, summarize what you told them, using strong final statements. Give them something they will remember, perhaps a call to action, something they should do in the next few days. Plan your ending so that your audience will remember you and your presentation.

Consider writing out your presentation and memorizing it the way an actor does his script. When a script is well memorized, the actor speaking it makes it sound as if the script's words are his own. The audience forgets that a script is being used because the actor is so comfortable with it. We all have sat in an audience so caught up in the performance that we forgot that it was all make-believe. When this happens, theater is at its most memorable and enjoyable. When I share tips and tools at the end of this chapter, I'll give you some ideas to help you memorize. If you feel you simply cannot memorize, remember that cue cards are a perfectly acceptable alternative.

So who should use a script? It could be the salesperson or telemarketer. The telemarketer is the worst because he tends to simply read his script and let the listener know he is reading it—what a turnoff! But other people can use scripts, too—managers, trainers, teachers, lawyers. And when you, too, have your script, it's time for the next step in preparing for the presentation—practice.

Practice

In theater, they call practice *rehearsal*. Actors rehearse many hours a week until their performance is perfect. You, too, can practice in many different ways. Try presenting to a friend or in front of a mirror. You can audiotape or videotape your presentation and critique yourself or ask someone you trust to give you feedback. Practice until your words become comfortable and become your own. You'll know when you are ready.

Even the best-prepared actor or presenter experiences fear before going onstage. This is normal, and it can even be helpful. Fear gets the adrenaline flowing and can make your brain sharper, so don't fight the fear—just don't let it paralyze you. Remain confident in yourself and in your knowledge that you are prepared and ready. Use relaxation techniques.

Visualize the performance in your head. Use visualization techniques to see how you want the performance to be. Tell yourself that it's all right if you are not perfect. Use your nervous energy to work for you, to help you to be the best you can be.

Use body language in your presentations

Have you ever sat in the last row of the theater, where it is impossible to see the faces of the actors? Nevertheless, you were able to understand what they were thinking and feeling. An actor is adept at using body language to communicate with the audience. This skill is crucial to success in business.

The ability to read your customer as well as the ability to use body language and words to sell your product or position is an important skill to possess.

Let's talk about the skills needed to sell yourself, your company, your idea, and your product or service. To be successful, we must be able to sell the only unique asset each of us has to offer—ourselves. To be successfully persuasive in getting your point across is of paramount importance.

You must learn how to read people if you want your customer—your audience—to buy what you are selling.

Body language, or nonverbal communication, has a significant effect on what you *actually* communicate versus what you *want* to communicate. How you move your body, head, limbs, and even fingers communicates a message, as do the speed, tone, and pitch of your voice. Even clothes, jewelry, and props convey a message. When you express emotions in a nonverbal way, your voice and body convey much about the way you are feeling. Just like an actor, learn to use your whole body to communicate. Try to understand what your subconscious may be thinking and feeling so that, in your communication, your body movements will align with your words.

Learn to read the body language of others to understand the deeper meaning of what they are really saying. When you feel a person is not telling the truth, look for signals in her body, voice, and words. Most research on communication states that it is 7 percent words, 38 percent tone of voice, and 55 percent body language.

TIPS AND TOOLS

Use your body and read others

Observe the posture, gestures, body movement, and facial expressions of others as well as the nonverbal elements of your own performance.

Body movement

Are you using your body's movements—as well as lack of movement—to communicate and to focus your audience's attention where you want it?

Gestures

Are you using your head and hands? Are your gestures compatible with what you are saying?

Posture

Is your stature alert and erect or are you slouching or too stiff?

Body language basics

Are your movements open, to convey acceptance or closed off?

Open and direct body language: This demonstrates a readiness and willingness to show emotions and feelings. It is characterized by a relaxed, warm posture, open arms, and animated facial expressions; a firm and friendly handshake; lots of nonverbal feedback when listening; sustained eye contact; use of many gestures and much voice intonation to make a point; is fast-paced, assertive, intense, and direct; and more people and relationship oriented.

Closed and self-contained body language: This demonstrates less willingness to show emotions and more control over thoughts and emotions. It is more formal and "proper" and is characterized by minimal physical contact and eye contact; crossed arms or legs; a formal or gentle handshake; limited facial expressions when talking or listening and minimal nonverbal feedback; is more understated, less direct, slow-paced, precise, courteous, reserved, easygoing, less assertive, and more task-oriented.

Deceitful or lying gestures: Many body language experts say that deceitful or lying gestures are characterized by touching the face or the mouth, especially on the left side, or by covering the mouth with a hand. Avoid these gestures unless you are trying to portray a deceitful character. Impatience is often portrayed by pacing back and forth.

Natural posture: Relax and stand upright with your shoulders back and your head held high, your feet slightly apart, and your arms loosely at your sides. Remember to breathe. Practice in front of a mirror until you look and feel comfortable. Plant your feet comfortably apart, and avoid rocking back and forth: this is a clear indication of nervousness and something you can easily do without knowing it. Make a concerted effort to be conscious of your feet.

Unnatural posture: This is characterized by hands clasped in front of the body or behind the back or hands in the pockets and rocking.

Gestures: They should appear natural and spontaneous. Use your hands to support what you are saying. Gesture with your hands to indicate size or direction; certain adverbs or verbs also lend themselves to gestures. However, avoid using the same gesture over and over.

Eye contact: Look at your audience; if possible, make eye contact with different people in the audience as you speak. If your audience is large, look at whole sections or groups of people. When you are making a presentation, eye contact is crucial.

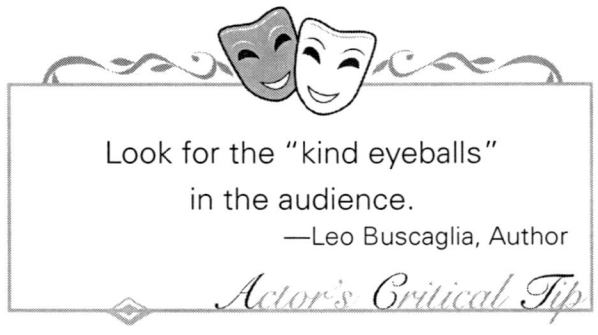

Look for the "kind eyeballs"
in the audience.
—Leo Buscaglia, Author

Actor's Critical Tip

During a presentation, I remember the advice from the late Leo Buscaglia, who wrote in his book *LOVE*, "look for the 'kind eyeballs' in your audience—the faces in the audience that are smiling at you, the people who are nodding their heads in agreement with what you are saying. This nonverbal encouragement and feedback will give you confidence and relax you, allowing you to draw on the energy of the audience, and in doing so, enhance your performance. The audience will return your excitement and enthusiasm every time."

Conversely, actors don't make eye contact with the audience (unless it is written into the script); instead, they look over the audience's heads to avoid breaking the "fourth wall" that separates the stage from the world outside it. Almost always, eye contact on stage is only with other actors. The next time you are attending a show and catch an actor sneaking a look at the audience, this should be a clear sign of an inexperienced or unprofessional actor.

Facial expressions

Are you smiling, or frowning? Is your face animated? Are you communicating interest using eye contact and gestures? Wear a happy, relaxed, and confident face regardless of what you are feeling inside. This will take practice—in front of a mirror is best.

Remember how as a kid, when someone was taking your picture, she asked you to say "Cheese!" to get you to relax your face and smile? Do what it takes to allow your face to mirror your emotions naturally. For example, a genuine smile will involve your eyes as well as your mouth. The more confident you are in your material, the more relaxed your face and body will be, allowing you to express real emotions. Practice is the best preparation for a relaxed presentation that will allow your body, posture, voice, gestures, and facial expressions to talk to your audience and align with the message you want to convey.

Involve all the senses

Again, Tony Jeary, in his book *Inspire Any Audience*, reiterates some interesting statistics on retention that most good presenters already know: how much the members of your audience remember and how much they will be inspired by what you say depends in part on how well you get all of their senses involved in experiencing your presentation. For example, as Jeary points out the average adult retains

- 10 percent of what he reads
- 20 percent of what he hears
- 30 percent of what he watches or sees
- 50 percent of what he hears and sees

- 70 percent of what he says aloud
- 90 percent of what he says, does, and teaches to someone else

In my presentations, I explain these statistics and ask participants to be sure to take notes. In fact, I often provide workbooks containing blank spaces and ask participants to fill in the blanks as they listen to me speak. I use flipcharts or PowerPoint presentations so that audience members can see words and images that illustrate my point. Often I will ask questions to get them talking and to repeat back what they learned.

At the end of my presentation, especially if the group is small, I often ask audience members to tell me one thing they learned and will put into practice immediately. To ensure the greatest possible retention among audience members, I also ask that they commit to telling—or, even better, teaching—someone else what they learned. I suggest to managers that if the expense of training is an issue, one participant should be sent to the training and be required to teach the others what they learned on their return. This ensures that maximum learning will take place for the participant because he knows he will need to teach others.

In our business environments and even in our personal lives, we will always need to present. There is an ever-present need to get on the stage and share what you have to offer with your audience. I clearly remember a fellow actor who was quite good on stage but who had a terrible fear of presenting to his colleagues at work. I coached him to use the skills he had as an actor in his job. He did so and overcame his stage fright in the business environment by approaching his presentations the same way he approached his part in the show. He memorized his script and practiced and visualized how he wanted the outcome to look. He went into his presentation telling himself that it was just another show, that his clients were his audience, that he was confident that he knew his material, and that he anticipated standing ovations and rave reviews.

Learning and thinking styles

It is not easy to memorize an eighty-page script, to remember where to stand as all your lines are delivered, to make sure that right props are in the right places, or to remember which costume you should wear in what scene. An actor has an incredibly large amount of information to learn and internalize in a relatively short time.

Learn how to identify learning and thinking styles and how to use that knowledge to help you learn, teach, present, and even sell to others. For example, whether you are a visual, auditory, or kinesthetic learner influences how easy learning will be for you (as well as for each member of every audience you play before). Understanding each style of learning and identifying your own personal style will help the process. You can then apply this knowledge in your business or personal environment.

In his book *The Power of Business Rapport,* Dr. Michael Brooks describes the importance of building rapport in everything you do. Drawing from a business environment, his book helps people as they try to influence, persuade, teach, present, and sell. Dr. Brooks refers to a process as Neurolinguistic Programming, or NLP (*neuro* = behavior, *linguistic* = language, programming = *altering actions*). His book, published in 1991, is now one of many books that teach the skills necessary to develop rapport with people in order to influence and persuade them. Dr. Brooks classifies people into three learning or thinking types: visual, auditory, and kinesthetic. I'll briefly explain NLP for you and outline the principles I've learned from Dr. Brooks and applied in my own life. If you're interested further, many good books have been written on this subject. I suggest you find one—it can be a very helpful tool.

Visual learners make up 55 percent of the population. Their experience is encoded through their eyes: what they see influences their behavior. They might think in terms of pictures and may speak using visual words and phrases such as "I see," "I can picture that," and "I get the picture." Using visual terms with this type of person can help you be more persuasive: "Can you see it?" "What would that look like?" "Picture this ...." "Can you see my point of view?" Visuals learn through observation and being shown what to do, rather than by being told.

Auditory learners, about 21 percent of the population, learn, think, and decide what to do by how things sound and can usually remember things that were said (or told) to them. They like the spoken word and can often be heard speaking to themselves. Sometimes ordinary background noise, of the type that wouldn't bother most other people, will bother an auditory learner. Auditory learners need to hear instructions: tell them what to do instead of writing it down. Verbal communication speaks volumes to them.

To sell or persuade an auditory learner, ask her to listen to you describe the good points of your product or service. Use auditory words: "Can you hear the sound that makes?" "What do you hear?" "Listen, doesn't that sound beautiful?" "Tell me; don't show me." "I hear what you're saying." "It's clear to me that we're in harmony." Let her talk, and listen when she does. Allow her to just listen when you talk, making sure you give verbal feedback as you do.

Kinesthetic learners, or feeling- and touch-based people, about 25 percent of the population, rely on feeling for their experiences. They are intimately connected to their feelings and extremely sensitive to those of others. These are the people who need to touch and feel things. They seem to have a "sense" about things and people. Talk to kinesthetics in terms of feelings, both yours and theirs, internal and external: "How do you feel about that?" "How does this make you feel?" "What are you feeling?" "I feel that ...." "I sense that ...." "Do you feel ready to ...?" "Deep down, I've got this gut feeling about ...." To be persuaded, kinesthetics need to feel a certain way about you and your service or product.

When you can conform yourself so that others experience you as a reflection of themselves, they begin to perceive you as charismatic.

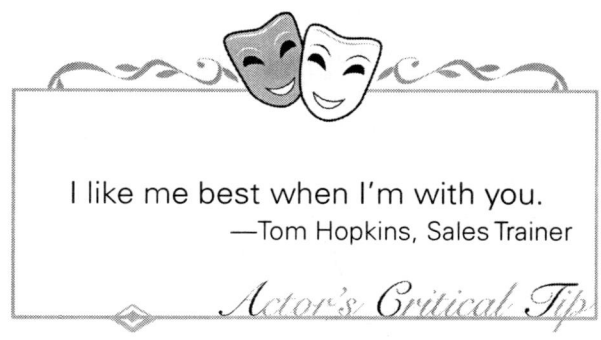

> I like me best when I'm with you.
> —Tom Hopkins, Sales Trainer

Actor's Critical Tip

So how do you know if you or another person is a visual, auditory, or kinesthetic learner? Dr. Brooks says to look for eye-accessing cues. According to him, the direction that people move their eyes is directly related to how they think. As the doctor points out, "People have to move their eyes to gain access to most representations." In other words, it is impossible to think at one's best without moving the eyes. Because the brain is incapable of doing two things at exactly the same instant, sustained eye contact breaks when a person does not know the answer to something and needs to think about it.

Dr. Brooks says that we can deduce a person's style by watching where his eyes go when he is looking away to think. Visuals look up when thinking. If they are remembering something, they will look up and to the left. Looking up and to the right indicates that a visual is accessing a visually constructed image or a visual picture of something that hasn't happened yet.

Auditories look sideways at eye level when thinking. When looking sideways to the left, an auditory is remembering something she once heard. When looking to the right, she is constructing an auditory perception or a sound she has not heard before.

Kinesthetics have only one position: down and to the right. (If a person is looking down and to the left, he is auditory and is having an internal dialogue, known as having a "third eye.")

Keep in mind that these clues apply to right-handed people. Lefties reverse the directions. Also, remember that directions are given from the person's perspective—her right, not yours. Here's how I use this information in a simple manner. When I am talking to someone and want to develop rapport, I notice the direction his eyes move when he is thinking: if up, then I know he's a visual; if sideways, an auditory; if down and to his right, a kinesthetic. I can then adjust my presentation accordingly to appeal to his senses.

You can use a simple test to determine someone's thinking and learning style. Ask him a question for which you know he won't immediately know the answer: for example, "What did you have for breakfast three days ago?" or "What was the name of your third-grade teacher?" If the person does not have to look away, he knows the answer without thinking, so come up with another question to ask. The answer is not what is important but rather that answering the question makes him think.

I have used this method to help teachers and parents figure out the learning styles of their students. Although in the past teachers used lecturing to get their points across, more and more teachers and college professors are recognizing that students have different styles and are thus incorporating visual, auditory, and kinesthetic presentation tools into their classrooms.

In the same way, this can be a useful tool to you during an interview or performance review. When I interview a person, I always ask, "Where do you see yourself in five years?" After asking the question, I watch her eyes. If she can look me in the eye without looking away and answers the question, that tells me that the person has previously thought about the answer and is probably goal-oriented. If she needs to look away and think about the answer, that tells me she may have not given prior thought to her long-term goals, which may be significant to me when hiring.

This knowledge can also be very helpful to you when you need to learn something new. Figure out what style you are, feel where you eyes go when thinking, and listen to the words you use: do you think in pictures or do you hear words? Discover your dominant style, and consider what style might be your secondary style.

For instance, I am definitely a visual learner with the kinesthetic style coming next and auditory last. I know I won't remember what someone tells me, so I always have a pen and paper with me to write down the things I need to remember. As an actor, this knowledge has served me well. Although I do not have a good memory for things, I can memorize very well. When I have a big part to memorize, I first look at the words over and over, saying them in my mind and then out loud, until I can see them in my mind. When I think I have the exact wording down, I make a tape of my lines and my cue lines, leaving a space after my cue. I then listen to the cue and repeat my line, seeing it in my head. Next, I listen to the line on tape to confirm that I am correct.

At the same time, when I am in rehearsals and I am on stage, the director gives me my blocking. By telling me where to stand when I say a particular line, he reinforces my kinesthetic style. I can feel where I am when I say each line. Knowing these things about how I learn allows me to use my knowledge to reinforce my learning, making it easy for me to remember both my lines and my blocking.

Take the time to learn how you learn and how the people with whom you interact learn and think. You will become more persuasive and more successful, not only in your professional life, but in everything you do.

In *The Experience Economy: Work Is Theater and Every Business a Stage*, Joseph Pine II and James H. Gilmore state it well when they say, "Work is theatre, and any business activity observed by a customer is nothing less than an act of theatre. No matter what position you hold in your company, you are a performer, and you must act accordingly. Actors should also avoid reminding the audience that they are acting. They must be able to stay in character so perfectly that observers never realize that they are on stage." Think about the last great movie or live play that you saw that engaged and engrossed you. As you watched the performance, did you see the actor as himself, or as the character he portrayed?

Practice and rehearsal are the only things that will make your presentation look natural and unrehearsed. You'll do the same thing over and over so that you can seem to be doing it for the first time. When great actors rehearse for hours on end, their performance seems so natural that the audience quickly forgets that the actor is acting, and the performance becomes believable, and engaging.

Remember: practice does not make perfect; perfect practice makes perfect. Your performance must be consistently perfect, each time. Study and practice until your material becomes your own, until it sounds comfortable and natural. After you have the material down pat, watch yourself in the mirror or audiotape or videotape yourself. Then ask friends or family to watch you (perhaps on YouTube) and give you constructive criticism.

Visualize the way you want the performance to be and practice, practice, practice. Learn to recognize visual clues about other people's thinking styles and at the same time know your own style of learning and decision making.

Everything you do communicates and sends a message. What you do with your body, your voice, and your words has an impact. Do you know what your body is saying? Does it match your intent? Just as a director gives his cast notes after each rehearsal to improve their performance, give yourself notes at the end of your day.

Debrief your presentation. Ask yourself the following questions: How did my performance go today? What did my audience think? What message did I send? Ask yourself and your audience (if you use evaluations) what you need to keep, discard, or create to improve your performance or enhance your results. Are there new ways you can delight, wow, or persuade your customers or clients?

Design your environment first in your head and then in reality, just like a director designs the set, the lighting, the costumes, and the props to deliver her message.

Only when you have done these things can you give the wonderful performance that will earn you rave reviews and keep your customers coming back for encore performances. You can do it!

I'm A
Brass   Band

RECOGNITION

Chapter 9

All kinds of music is pouring out of me, 'Cause ... somebody loves me at last!

Recognition

("I'm a Brass Band" from *Sweet Charity*
—Lyrics by Dorothy Fields)

Ah, the smell of the greasepaint and the roar of the crowd. This is what the actor thrives on—especially the roar of the crowd. There is nothing like hearing thunderous applause for a job well done. To look out at the audience from the stage and see those smiling faces, the hands clapping, and perhaps some people standing brings a swell of pride and a sense of achievement that are unequaled.

I remember watching the Academy Awards one year and thinking how thrilling it must be to stand before friends, family, and colleagues to be recognized for a job well done. In my acting career, I have been fortunate to be awarded for excellence in acting a few times, and believe me, the feeling is every bit as wonderful as you can imagine. And then I asked myself: is it possible for everyone to know the joy of being recognized and rewarded for the work she does? It's not as difficult as it seems. The challenge is discovering how to make it happen.

One of the reasons I wrote this book was to give people who might never stand on stage a chance to hear that applause and to experience that feeling. And we all could, if we all had the skills necessary to understand what recognition looks like in our everyday world. I'll never forget when Sally Field, in 1985, while accepting her second Oscar in five years as Best Actress for her role in *Places of the Heart*, said to her audience, "You like me. You really like me!" The pride she felt for being recognized and respected was obvious and heartwarming. This is a feeling we all long for, knowing we are liked and appreciated for our efforts and achievements.

I hope to help you learn how to accept all forms of praise and recognition from others, how to give it to others, and even how to give it to yourself.

I recently taught my young, aspiring actor and granddaughter, Maya, what a "standing ovation" means. She now says, "When the people on the stage do a really good job, then at the end of the play the people in the audience will stand up and clap. The audience will always clap, but if they stand up that means you were really good."

How will Maya recognize applause and standing ovations in her everyday life? What must her parents, grandparents, and teachers do to make sure that Maya, her brother, Aiden, and her sister, Lyla, know that every day they do things that merit recognition, applause, and standing ovations? What will a job well done look like in their world? What does it look like in your world?

Earlier, when I discussed leadership, I described how a director recognizes the cast long before they get applause and standing ovations from the audience. An effective director gives constant recognition and encouragement in the form of notes after each rehearsal. He should mention first the things done well and only after that the things the actor can do to improve his performance or his understanding of his character. Consistent small acts of praise and recognition keep actors moving forward and help them be open to constructive criticism. In other words, first catch somebody doing something right.

When I was in college studying to be a teacher, I remember being taught that during a parent–teacher conference, the teacher should always start by saying something good about the student and end by doing the same thing. Both of these strategies leave the parents open to hear suggested improvement opportunities for their child when it is placed strategically in the middle of the conversation.

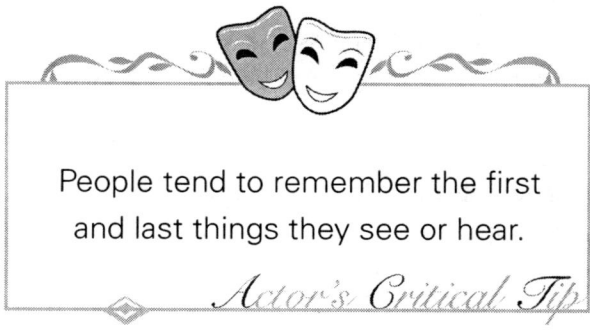

People tend to remember the first
and last things they see or hear.

Actor's Critical Tip

Proper recognition of employees can also yield powerful results. Leaders and managers need to both identify and provide the type of recognition and reward that will motivate employees to perform at their highest levels of capability and skill. But even though understanding the importance of positive recognition is important in the business world, unfortunately, many leaders do not believe in recognition: performing is part of the job, and why should an employee be recognized for simply doing his job? Some leaders even believe that recognition will only make employees lazy. I actually heard a manager say to a group of employees he overheard commenting that they rarely hear a nice word from the boss, "If you want applause, join the circus."

In this book, I've recommended the book *Fish!*, a corporate training video and management parable based on Seattle's Pike Place Fish Market. It's a place where employees toss fish to customers—sort of the Southwest Airlines of fishmongers. *Fish!* talks about the value of fun in the workplace and asserts that employees are more effective when they are enjoying their jobs, having fun, and being recognized for the good work they do. Fun and recognition can go hand in hand in any organization.

Once a director on receiving the Academy Award for Best Director, commented that a director's job is filling everyone with the desire to come back to work at 10 AM the next morning. Isn't this the job of every leader? Sadly, recognition and fun are not priorities for many managers who feel that a paycheck is recognition enough for an employee. Perhaps they fear that recognition can come to be seen an entitlement, something that employees expect for every action. If they do, they're confusing *rewards* and *recognition*. Recognition has little financial cost; it requires only awareness and time from managers and ensures long-term results.

So why recognize employees? In this day and age, when unemployment is so high, the competition for the best and most-skilled employees has never been greater. Research tells us that pay and benefits are the top two reasons why candidates accept any job, but these two things will not retain people forever. More than money, people want to be valued, appreciated, and recognized. These things retain employees when paychecks alone cannot.

Each of the series of studies called *What Workers Want*, conducted by Lawrence Lindahl in the 1940s, Ken Kovach in the 1980s, and Bob Nelson in the 1990s, reported similar findings: managers rated "good wages, job security, promotion, and growth opportunities" as the highest employee motivators, whereas employees rated "full appreciation for work done, feeling 'in' on things, and sympathy to personal problems" as their actual greatest motivators. Similarly, Aon Consulting Workforce Commitment Index in Ann Arbor, Michigan, stated that "pay and benefits are the top two reasons for accepting a position, but the power of pay and benefits is only strong during the recruitment stage."

In a survey by William M. Mercer, Inc., recognition for a job well done was the top motivator of employee performance with money coming in a close second. Compensation attracts employees, but recognition retains them.

In chapter five on leadership, I outlined why people fail: lack of knowledge and lack of motivation. Motivation can begin with recognition. Ask employees what types of recognition would motivate them and match that type of recognition to that employee. Remember, however, that recognition must support the behaviors and goals of the organization as well as the employee's sense of self-worth. And keep in mind that recognition is most effective when given as soon as possible after deserving behavior.

Do not confuse recognition with reward. Good leaders manage by walking around and catching someone doing something well. An immediate "Thank you" or "Good job!" encourages others to keep performing well. Recognize employees in both formal and informal settings to produce the full effect. When employees are recognized in public, other employees get clear examples of what is valued in the organization.

It is also important to remember, and effective leaders know, that all recognition and rewards should be done formally and in public, providing the employee is comfortable with public recognition, while criticism should be done one on one in private.

> People respond to your behavior.
> they do not know what your feelings
> are; they only see your behavior.
> —Dr. Joy Brown, Author
>
> *Actor's Critical Tip*

I repeat what has been said time and again: people would rather be praised than criticized, but will often take criticism over being ignored. It's hard to believe that bad news is often preferred over no news. The two-year-old would rather be recognized than punished but will always choose being punished over being ignored. Why do you think the tantrums are usually in public places?

Tantrums will almost always generate attention from the parent, and when attention is received, the negative behavior is reinforced.

The same principle applies to grownups. We all crave attention—preferably positive, in the form of recognition—and will do whatever it takes to get it.

Think about your workplace and what happens when something goes wrong, a mistake is made, or someone fails. Does that person or group get attention from a manager? You bet. A meeting is called, and everyone is read the riot act and told that we will *not* repeat that behavior. Then, when the behavior is not repeated, when things go well and people do things right, is anything heard from management? More often than not, no. Nothing is said to recognize the behavior that produced good results, only what produced bad results.

Thus, many times the only time we get the attention we crave is when we mess up. So what do we do, albeit unconsciously? Some might say we mess up again to get some attention.

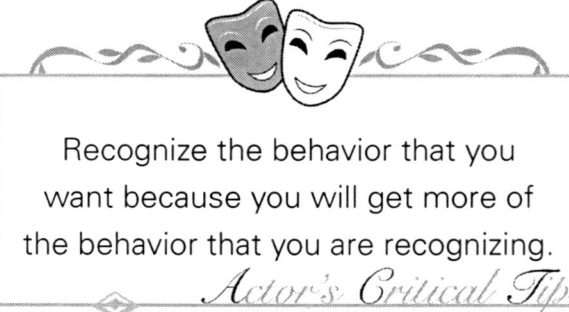

Recognize the behavior that you want because you will get more of the behavior that you are recognizing.

Actor's Critical Tip

That's why behavior modification experts tell parents to catch a kid doing something right and recognize that behavior. The more we ignore inappropriate behavior and recognize appropriate behavior, the more we will get appropriate behavior. Recognize the behavior you want in someone, and you'll likely get more of that behavior in return.

Bob Nelson, in his book *1001 Ways to Reward Employees*, says, "We know from 100 years of research that behavior is shaped by consequences. If you recognize and reward behavior, it will tend to be repeated. If you ignore or punish behavior, it will tend to stop. In short, you get what you reward." Nelson, like the behavior experts, states, "Catch them doing something right. It's surprising how many companies don't see the importance of recognizing outstanding employee performance. Yet studies show that such recognition is a huge motivator for workers. And often it's free!" Multiply loyalty, energy, and good work from employees by paying close attention and simply seeing them do something right.

TIPS AND TOOLS

We can get the idea of the value of recognition of employees simply by visiting a bookstore or going online and seeing the hundreds of books written on the subject. Remember that one of the most effective ways of developing a recognition process is to involve the people in the organization in its creation, only then will you really know what your employees' value and what will motivate them. Having said that, I'll share a few ideas I've encountered that have been effective. The recognition processes I'll describe have little or no cost involved; the reward programs, on the other hand, will incur some cost.

Recognition programs

Employee teams: Form a team of employees to develop a reward and recognition process. For example, SouthTrust Bank at one time included employees in decisions concerning employee recognition and charitable giving. SouthTrust reported that it improved its employee satisfaction by two percentage points in two years, as reported by an independent study.

Recognition by management: If you are in management, call your team into your office. Watch the reactions of the employees. Usually you'll see fear or anxiety and hear whispers: "What did we do wrong now?" When all are assembled, smile and go around the room, saying to each team member, "I want you to know that I value you because ...." Mention something good you observed her doing, then continue until you've done this for the entire team in front of each other. Now observe the team members' behavior for the rest of the day, and the week, even the month that follows. You will be amazed how much positive effect your sincere, kind words will have on future behavior. The message you've sent is very clear: *The boss is watching what we do and is looking for the good stuff, too. In fact, he'll even take time out of his busy day to tell me that I did a good job.* You will reap the rewards of this practice.

The only difficult part is remembering to start managing by walking around and looking for good things instead of bad, finding something different for each employee. This activity costs only time, and it pays big dividends.

Someone special: Many companies are using this method now. American Airlines used to have "You're Someone Special" cards around the airport. When a customer experienced an exceptional act of service by an employee, she could present one of these cards to that employee. Customers also had the option of mailing the cards to corporate headquarters. Ultimately, employees received recognition of superior performance in front of their peers.

Magic moments or WOW moments: These allow customers and fellow employees to recognize someone. Employees and guests complete a Magic Moment or WOW card each time an employee provides service above and beyond the call of duty. Employees who receive noticeably high levels of recommendation may earn certificates, gold lapel pins, days off, and so forth.

Recognition exercise: Distribute the form below to employees to complete and ask that they include their name. This exercise was suggested by Joe Hamby, a colleague of mine, who reports having great success with the process.

1. Would you expect recognition for your outstanding accomplishment? If so, why?
2. If so, how would you like to be recognized?

3. If you were to receive an award or reward, what would the award look like?
4. What criteria should be used to make a recognition process effective?
5. Who should recognize employees: management, fellow employees, customers?
6. If you were to receive a monetary reward, what would you do with the money?

Employees' answers to the questions will give you good insight into your employees and what they value. The last question is interesting as it provides information as to what motivates someone. Time off is now highly valued. In the hectic, time-consuming world in which we live, having more time to spend with friends and family has become an effective motivator.

Feedback from this exercise will be helpful in developing an effective recognition process, and it encourages employee participation, leading to employee buy-in. Below are some interesting answers employees have given to the listed questions, including ones that require very little or no outlay of money.

Awards recommended by employees

Plaque displayed where employees and customers can see it
Thank-you note
Pat on the back (both privately and publicly)
Dinner or a movie for two
Certificate of appreciation
Parking space for the month
Cash award
Breakfast or lunch with a manager or owner
Free car wash and gasoline fill-up
Name and picture in the company newsletter or local newspaper
Time off with pay
Name on company marquee
Name and reason for recognition prominently displayed

A trip
Business cards
Gift certificate
Trophy
Name tag with special designation of team or contribution

Shirt with name and contribution (for example, the team member's name and the process he contributed to improving)

Letters in paychecks: When an employee or employee team works on creating a process, a wonderful way to recognize them is for the owner or senior management team to write a thank-you letter describing the thing the team or person worked on and how favorable the outcome was. Then include the letter in all of the employees' paychecks to give the note added importance and to be sure it is read.

Reward programs

STARS program: This is adapted from the Doubletree Hotel's goal that every employee should know every customer's name. Customers' names are on their credit card, on their reservation information, and so on. Managers reinforce and reward by carrying chips engraved with stars. When a manager hears an employee using a customer's name, she gives a chip to the employee. At the end of the week or month, the employee trades in his chips for silver dollars or dollar bills at a rate of one to one. Many variations on this theme are possible—for example, replacing chips with dollars straight out, asking employees a given customer's name with the same prospect of reward. As other employees observe this interaction, whether they are the employee being rewarded or not, they observe desired behaviors. This process, and variations on it, can be used to encourage progress toward any goal through a variety of desired behaviors.

Monthly rewards: Hold a sales contest. Purchase three prizes and display prizes where employees can see them each day. At the end of the month, the winning employee chooses one of the three available prizes, which is replaced with a different prize to make another set of three prizes for the next month.

Daily rewards: Monthly goals can be broken into daily increments. This can be a sales contest or one based on any daily desired outcome. The winner will receive a gift certificate to a local restaurant or place of business. With a little effort, it is easy to get local merchants who are looking to support the community and drive business for themselves to donate prizes.

Management reward and recognition: Starting with your yearly budget or expected profit as a point of reference, develop levels of success above and beyond the goal. If the company succeeds, managers earn bonuses. Such a program promotes teamwork among department managers to identify opportunity areas and develop solutions.

Suggestion boxes: Use suggestion boxes to gather ideas and to recognize employees' ideas and contributions. This is a variation on normal suggestion boxes, which often contain employee problems and gripes. I call it The Solution Box. All suggestions are welcome, but each suggestion or problem must be accompanied by a proposed solution. Reward the employee who provides the best solution.

Another variation is for management to post problems, things that need fixing, and areas of opportunity within the organization in a place where employees can see them. Employees may then submit solutions they like to any of the published problems or weaknesses. Reward and recognize each employee publicly when her solution is adopted or adapted.

Catch someone doing something right: Managers can recognize and reward employees when they notice them doing a great job. Employees can receive stars, coins, or certificates or variations on the rewards previously described. Employees can recognize coworkers in the same way.

Wheel of fortune: In a variation of the television game show, set a goal for employees to meet. Employees spin the wheel monthly when they meet their goal and receive the prize the wheel lands on. Prizes could be monetary or take the form of merchandise or services. Both large and small items can be included—perhaps spa days, iPods, DVD players, movie tickets, dinners, gift certificates, or anything else fun or unusual.

Employee of the day/week/month: We have all experienced programs like this. To be creative about who votes and about what the reward should be, ask employees for suggestions and refer to the rewards suggested by employees.

I recommend two books by John Putzier. One is called *Get Weird: 101 Innovative Ways to Make Your Company a Great Place to Work.* The other is *Weirdoes in the Workplace!—Love 'Em, Leave 'Em or Lose 'Em!* John devotes many chapters to what he calls, "weird ideas for perks, pay, and pats on the back"—in other words, recognition and incentives.

John says in *Get Weird* that "a lack of suitable recognition and rewards is cited as a leading cause of employee dissatisfaction and turnover, so if you make some strides in recognition, you will automatically improve your chances of keeping good people." John goes on to say that "compensation is not the only variable in successful employee recruitment, retention, and motivation. If there is one employee need that seems to be universal, however, it is to be recognized for a job well done or even for something totally unrelated to one's direct output, like maybe a birthday." John's books contain wonderful, funny, and, yes, even weird ideas that can be used effectively in any business.

The possible variations on recognition and reward programs are endless. Be creative, involve employees, and open yourself up to having some fun. You'll be amazed at the increase in employee loyalty, morale, and production you see as well as the customer satisfaction and profitability your business enjoys. The important thing to understand is that how you recognize and reward employees is less important than that you do so.

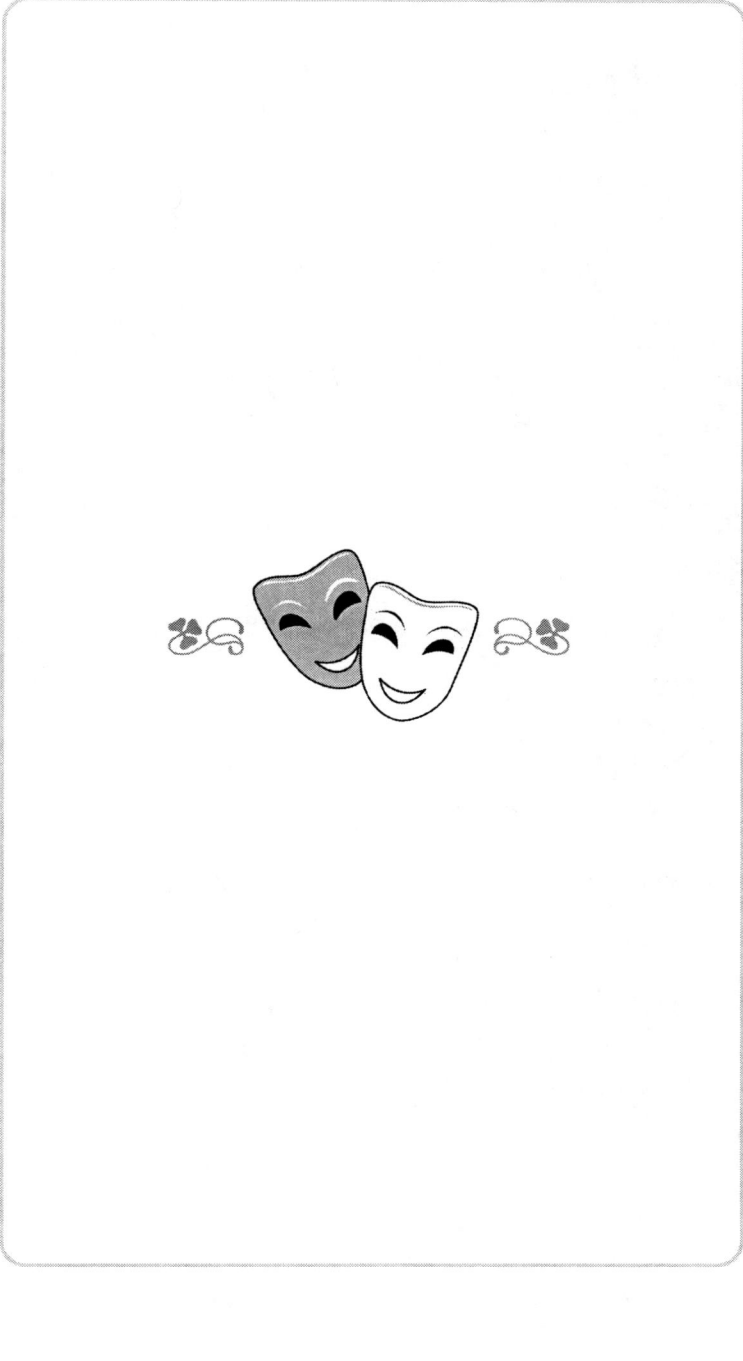

Happy Talk

COMMUNICATIONS SKILLS

Chapter 10

Happy talk, keep talkin', happy talk, Talk about things you'd like to do

Communication Skills

("Happy Talk" from *South Pacific*
—Lyrics by Oscar Hammerstein II)

Communication is the key to success in any business. As an actor and a professional business consultant, I recognize this fact. On the stage, the actor must communicate with the audience and bring its members along on a journey as the show progresses. Unless actors effectively communicate with the audience, the show will fail, and the same holds true in business. If employees and managers cannot effectively communicate with each other or with customers or clients, the business will not succeed.

As a business consultant, I have concluded that when a business, relationship, or individual is not achieving set goals, it is usually because of a deficiency in the area of communication. Conversely, when success is being achieved, the company or individual is often proficient in communication skills. In my opinion, the ability to effectively communicate is a prerequisite for success. And failure to communicate can be costly to companies. Studies show that communication mishaps erode productivity and leave employers at a competitive disadvantage.

For example, a study done by OfficeTeam points out that executives say that 14 percent of each forty-hour work week is wasted because of poor communication between staff and management. That amounts to a staggering seven work weeks of lost productivity a year. And it's not without cause: phone calls have replaced much of face-to-face communication, and e-mails and texts further reduce personal interactions between people.

Often poor communication from upper management is a problem frequently linked to emotionally charged situations at work. In the absence of facts, rumor and innuendo fill the gap. Morale frequently improves when communication improves. One chairman of an executive communications group said, "People don't resist change, they resist the unknown."

It seems fitting to me that I am writing this final chapter of my book after finishing a run of one of my favorite shows, playing in what was certainly my favorite part. The show was *Crossing Delancey*, and I played the part of Bubbie, an eighty-something Jewish grandmother from New York. This show epitomizes how theater communicates. The story centers around a devoted granddaughter, Isabelle (Izzy, as she prefers to be called), who visits weekly with her elderly grandmother, Bubbie, on the lower east side of Manhattan. Izzy is infatuated with a local author, but Bubbie and her matchmaker friend, Hannah, have other plans. The story unfolds as Bubbie and Hannah try to interest Izzy in Sam the pickle man, who is steadfast, attentive, and the perfect match—in Bubbie's eyes.

It is a beautiful, sentimental, romantic comedy with many messages worth communicating. In the program, the director, Cindi East, wrote, "The last few years have been so tough for so many of us, and this play is a welcome respite. Its warmth and humor leave us feeling happy and hopeful, and while the obvious message is about finding love, the subtext gives us a lesson in humility, acceptance, and the importance of family and familial history."

One of the reasons I love theater so much is that it gives me an avenue to communicate with an audience to have my message heard.

One of the traditions of the Chino Community Theater, where *Crossing Delancey* was staged, is that after the performance, the cast goes outside immediately to greet the audience. In most community theaters, the cast members change out of their costumes and makeup before they go out to greet their guests. Usually by then, the only people waiting are friends and family. At first I thought the tradition at this theater to go out in costume was strange—that it might even ruin the magic of theater. However, my mind was changed very quickly as each night I stood outside greeting audiences of strangers as well as friends and family.

As actors, we know our friends and family will usually say wonderful things about our performances, but when strangers stand in line to get a chance to talk to you and thank you for making them feel or remember something from their past, the feeling is amazing. Every night as I stood outside in my grandmother costume, makeup, and graying hair, audience members, most of them people I had never met before, came up to me—or, rather, came up to Bubbie—and, without reservation, both men and women, hugged me and thanked me. Many said that the character brought back memories of their mother or grandmother, some of whom had passed on. Often they teared up as they told me stories of their grandmothers' coming from the old country and bringing warmth, love, and special foods into their lives. It was obvious that we had communicated to these people and that they had clearly received the messages that the play's author, director, and cast had set out to convey. To communicate on this level is a wondrous feeling and is the reason that acting brings me such joy.

Actress and songwriter Debra Harris, talking about communication, says, "To build credibility, motivate others, and unleash greater creativity, you must master the skills of communication before you can make meaningful changes." Acting is the ultimate form of communication. It starts with understanding what the author of the play wanted to say through the script. Then the director communicates the author's vision of the show to the cast. The actors then communicate to the audience through their performances. The audience communicates back through applause, standing ovations, and spoken and written accolades.

As I explained at the beginning of this book, my intent has been to examine how the skills used by actors can be learned and then practiced in everyday life, both in business and in our personal lives. How, what, and to whom do you need to communicate daily? How effective is your communication? Do you find yourself having to repeat instructions or requests over and over? Do you often feel as if people are not listening to you? You may be partially to blame: you may not be communicating in a way that can be heard.

Effective communication is a two-way process. The ability to speak effectively, to speak so that you are really heard, is necessary and so is the ability to actively and effectively listen. Take the time to learn and practice both skills. In theater, as in life, communication is both verbal and nonverbal. You are always communicating—sometimes verbally, always nonverbally.

Albert Mehrabian, Professor Emeritus of Psychology at UCLA, has become best known for his publications on the relative importance of verbal and nonverbal messages. His findings have been quoted in human communication seminars worldwide and have become known as the *7%-38%-55% rule.*

In his studies, he sought to discover how people decide whether they like one another and concludes the following:

Total liking = 7% verbal liking + 38% vocal liking + 55% facial liking

He generalizes this to mean that in all communications

- 7 percent happens through spoken words
- 38 percent happens through voice tone
- 55 percent happens through general body language

Other tests point to the possibility that 60 percent of communication is body language, 30 percent voice, and 10 percent words that contribute to the communication of attitudes. I touched on this in an earlier chapter when we discussed presentations. The percentages are less important than the point, which is that most communication takes place nonverbally.

What comprises nonverbal communication? Actors learn how to align their body language with their words, as well as how to express emotions through nonverbal communication. Gestures, whether using the hands, the legs, the head, or whole-body positioning, convey a message. Nonverbal signals are used to manage control of who is speaking. Interrupting, speaking louder or faster, and leaning toward or away from someone while speaking or listening all send messages. Practicing these techniques can be helpful in everyday life. Use your body, voice, and words to communicate, be aware of what your subconscious is saying through your body language, and watch others to read deeper meaning into what they say or do not say.

Nonverbal communication, both onstage and off, is also communicated by the environment. What do we see and hear around us? The director communicates messages in the set: the furniture, the pictures, and the knickknacks all send a message. In theater, "dressing the set" is deciding everything that will be on stage, where it will be placed, how it will be used, and its accessibility to the actor who will use it. Every prop and set piece has significance to the play and its actors, even if the audience is not consciously aware of that significance.

Costumes, jewelry, neatness, and personal grooming are also used to communicate with audiences, sometimes in obvious ways (like when I used makeup and hair color to age myself as Bubbie) and sometimes in less obvious ways. What does your "costume"—the way you dress—communicate to others? What message does your environment, your office, or your home convey to others? If your office is messy and littered with papers or tools, what message are you conveying to your boss? Remember that what you wear and what you surround yourself with communicates who you are—and the message is very clear.

Today's advertisers and designers spend considerable time and money to determine the effects of color on prospective buyers. Color is used in hospitals, business offices, and institutions in an attempt to influence behavior and communicate messages. Similarly, we are all aware of how music communicates. Try watching a play or movie or television show, and observe how the background music is used to convey a mood or message.

Communication comes in many forms, each of which can be effective in its own way and time. Become attuned to the means of your communication. Face-to-face communication offers opportunities for many nonverbal cues. Phone calls offer nonverbal messages through tone and volume of voice, pitch, sounds (like sighs or grunts), and pauses. Even silences can speak volumes. In sales, it is well-known that after you ask a closing question, you shut up: the first person who speaks loses.

Written communications offer more nonverbal signals than you might imagine. Aren't we all aware that using caps in e-mail indicates yelling? Handwriting, typeface, our use of spaces, color, and emoticons all send nonverbal messages. If you write a poorly written letter or a letter that is smudged or that has words crossed out, what are you telling its reader?

Communication is unavoidable. It is impossible to *not* communicate. To improve your communication, become aware of what your body, your voice, and your words are saying, and learn to interpret these clues in others.

A discussion on communication would not be complete without a discussion of listening. Many actors will tell you that the thing that makes a scene work is the art of listening to the other actors. Actor Eugene Levy says, "A scene moves forward by talking and listening with other people. Listening is as important as talking. You should know when to stand there and listen and not break the moment trying to go for something."

But many of us listen "with our motors running"—not really listening at all but just waiting for our turn to speak.

Really *listening* is a difficult skill that actors must practice and ultimately perfect. When you finally are at the point where you know your lines cold, you can begin to stop thinking about your next line and listen instead to the other actors saying their lines. If you do not master this, it could be a disaster when another actor says the wrong line or gives you the wrong cue. If you are not listening, you may deliver a line that is correct but that makes no sense in the new context.

Learning to really listen to others ensures that your message will be clear even if the lines that precede it are compromised. Actor and comedienne Catherine O'Hara said about Christopher Guest, actor, writer, and director for the mockumentary *Waiting for Guffman*, "The only note Chris gave me, before I even opened my mouth on *Waiting for Guffman*, was, 'Don't be afraid to listen.' And it is such a good reminder: just listen. In life, you have to listen." The author of *Lifeskills*, Dr. Redford Williams, made this profound statement: "You aren't really listening unless you are willing to be changed by what you hear."

Active and effective listening is a skill each of us must learn and practice. Psychologists know that humans spend 80 percent of their waking hours communicating. Only 45 percent, or twenty-seven minutes per hour, is spent listening. Worse, only 25 percent, or seven minutes per hour, is devoted to active or effective listening.

Why is listening so difficult?

- We think faster than we talk. People speak at a speed of 180 words per minute but have the ability to listen at a rate of 300–500 words per minute. This leaves us plenty of time for internal dialogue or daydreaming while someone else is talking.
- We listen with our motors running, just waiting for our turn to respond and preparing what we are going to say. And when we do this, we miss vital information. Sometimes we are so busy with ourselves inside our own heads that we do not hear the other person at all.

- Emotional filters keep us from hearing what we don't want to hear. This is a good reason to take someone with you when you go to the doctor's office and need to really hear what the doctor is saying.

- We assume that listening is a passive process. We must assume responsibility for actively listening.

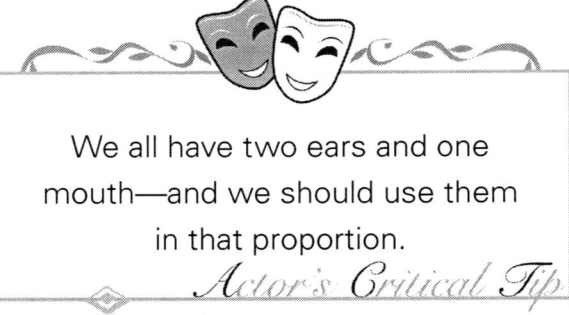

We all have two ears and one
mouth—and we should use them
in that proportion.

Actor's Critical Tip

To effectively and actively listen,

- Listen twice as much as you talk

- Only interrupt to get clarification

- Listen as if you will have to give feedback or repeat what you heard

- Repeat what you heard to check for understanding

- Ask open-ended questions

- Observe the body language of the speaker

- Look at the speaker and make good eye contact

- Jot down some notes about what you hear to keep yourself engaged

Remember that when you are speaking, you cannot be listening; thus, in saying too much, you hear too little.

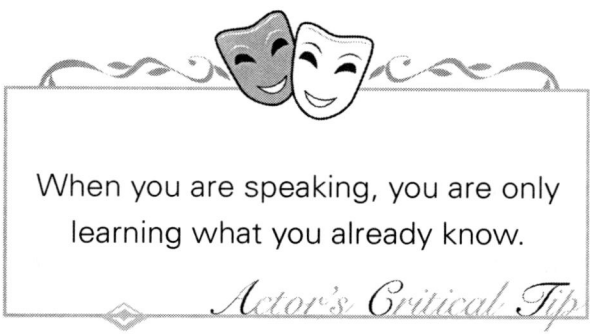

When you are speaking, you are only
learning what you already know.

Actor's Critical Tip

In addition, it is important to be an effective speaker when you communicate. When you speak because you want an action to be taken, you are coaching. Coaching is about communicating what you want to have done. It is about speaking with your words, body, and voice so that people will listen and understand. I once read a study that said 94 percent of college students admitted that they did not understand the professor at least twice in a given class period. And 70 percent said they would not ask for clarification out of a fear of being conspicuous or looking stupid. Too often we learn early on not to question when we do not understand or hear accurately.

If you often have to repeat things or it seems as if people are not listening to you, you may not be speaking effectively. To be an effective speaker is to be an effective coach. Explain what you want to communicate or what you want done, then demonstrate it, then let listeners do it, then observe them doing it and give them feedback on it.

Ultimately, who takes the main responsibility for success in communication? Is it the sender/speaker or the listener? Most would say it is the speaker. But 80 percent of success in communication depends on the listener, and only 20 percent on the speaker.

Successful communication is based on the ability to listen, to understand the needs, to ask open-ended questions for clarification, and to observe nonverbal messages. Steven Covey, author of *The Seven Habits of Highly Successful People* says "Our #1 need is to be heard."

TIPS AND TOOLS

Law of primacy and recency

Primacy: People remember the first thing they hear.

Recency: People remember the most recent thing they've heard.

Questions that can be used to move the conversation, check for understanding, and open communication

Tell me more.

Please help me; it gets lonely without any feedback.

Let me see if I understand:

Did I hear you say …?

Are you saying that …?

Could you expand on that?

Please explain.

How does that work?

Does everyone agree?

Is that all?

Is there anything else?

Does anyone have a different idea?

Why is that?

And that means …?

Did everyone understand that?

Your goal should be to communicate the following message: *This is what I think you are saying (or feeling). Am I right or wrong?*

Watch a television interview or a public speaker

Does the speaker's body language sync with his words?

What do his facial expressions say?

What does his voice convey?

Listen without sound. Can you understand the general mood of the person?

Effective speaking exercise

Rules: No questions

Instructions:

- Draw two parallel lines
- At one end of those parallel lines, connect the lines with an upside-down letter V.
- Connect the other end of the parallel lines with a straight line.
- On one side of the upside-down V, draw two more parallel lines.
- Connect one end of these lines with a straight line.

Debrief:

Say the following:

Look at each other's drawings; are they all alike? (In most cases the drawings will not be the same.)

Why are the drawings different?

Did you not all hear the same instructions?

Were you listening? Were you trying to succeed?

Whose fault is it that the group did not succeed? (Most people will say it was their own fault, and some will blame failure on the speaker due to the inability to ask questions.)

Then explain that the group failed because YOU, the speaker, did not do a good job of communicating.

Repeat the exercise:

New Rules: Same instructions. This time allow and encourage questions by saying, *Any questions?* When someone asks a question say, *Good question.* Some examples of questions asked: *Are lines horizontal or vertical? How long are the lines? How far apart?* (The drawings will begin to look similar but not everyone will succeed.)

Debrief:

What was different the second time?

What did I do differently?

What did you do differently?

Whose fault is it that not everyone succeeded?

(Participants may blame themselves at this point. Tell them that their failure is still your fault.)

Repeat the exercise:

Draw a simple house with a chimney. Describe how it should look. Draw an example along with the group. Check for understanding.

Draw two parallel lines: the sides of the house.

At one end of the parallel lines, connect the lines with an upside-down V. This is the roof of the house.

Connect the other side with a straight line: this is the bottom of the house.

On one side of the upside-down V, draw two more parallel lines: this is the chimney.

Connect one end of these lines with a straight line: this is the top of the chimney.

Debrief by asking the group:

What was different the third time?

Why did we succeed?

Why did all the drawings look different the first time?

Here are some possible answers:

First time:

- No questions were allowed
- Directions were vague
- No modeling was given

Second time:

Why did the drawings get better the second time?

Questions were allowed and encouraged

How were questions encouraged?

- The speaker asked, *Are there any questions?* (After a question was asked, the speaker responded with, *Good question* to encourage more questions.)

Third time:

Why did the group all succeed and draw the same house the third time?

- Questions were allowed and encouraged
- The desired outcome/goal was clear to all
- The outcome (the house) was modeled by the speaker, there was a demonstration of what the final result should look like

Learn how to speak so that people will listen to and understand you. To coach or speak effectively, communicate so that your listeners can understand.

Listening exercise

Separate a group into pairs. One person in each pair is the speaker, the other the listener.

Speaker: Talk for sixty seconds about your life history.

Listener: No notes, no interruptions, and be prepared to repeat back what you heard.

Debrief:

How many speakers had difficulty talking about themselves?

How many listeners wanted to interrupt?

Say:

If you wanted to interrupt but didn't, you demonstrated good listening and self-discipline.

Was it difficult to focus on someone else and really hear the story?

Did it feel good to be heard?

Have the listener repeat the story back so that the speaker can check for understanding.

Ask: *How much did the listener hear correctly and entirely?*

Reverse the roles and repeat the exercise.

The listeners will usually be able to repeat back almost all of what they heard.

Ask: *Why were the listeners successful and able to repeat back what they heard?*

Possible answers:

I was really focused on the speaker.

I listened carefully and actively because I knew I would have to repeat back what I heard.

Debrief lesson learned:

Always listen as if you will need to feedback what you heard and then do so, that way the speaker knows they were heard and understood.

Avoid mushroom management

The *Urban Dictionary* as well as many books and articles on leadership and communication cite the concept of mushroom management as "an allusion to a company's staff being treated like mushrooms: kept in the dark, covered with dung, and when grown big enough, canned (fired)." The connotation is that management is making decisions without consulting the staff affected by those decisions and possibly not even informing the staff until well after the decisions are made. This phenomenon is most commonly found in organizations that have a strict hierarchy as well as barriers to cross-organizational communication, but it can be found in any organization. The negative results of this lack of communication can be devastating to an organization. For better results, practice the following guiding principles for communication.

Guiding principles for communication

1. Focus all comments on the situation, issue, or behavior, not on the person. This technique eliminates defensiveness:

I understand the emotion, but the behavior is inappropriate.

2. Protect the self-confidence and self-esteem of others. Positive recognition should be communicated in public and negative communication in private.

3. Protect relationships with employees, peers, and managers, communicating and listening effectively to increase morale.

4. Be proactive; take the first step to making things better. Encourage listening; be a better listener to others.

5. Be an example to others. Listen actively and model the behavior you are looking for in others.

Remember Steven Covey's words in *The Seven Habits of Highly Effective People*:

"Seek first to understand, then to be understood."

Use the skills the actor uses
on your own stage—
the stage of life.

Actor's Critical Tip

A Message from the Author

Dear Reader,

I hope you have found my message to be valuable. I have been true to my mission if you have learned at least one new fact, skill, or behavior that will help you move closer to your full potential.

As you go forward remember to ask yourself:

- What is my stage?
- What is my role in the show?
- Who is my audience?
- Did I earn a standing ovation?
- Will I get rave reviews and recommendations?
- Will my audience (customers) demand encore performances?

I have a request of you. Would you be willing to help me spread the message of *Getting Your Act Together* so more people can learn *How to Put the SHOW into Business*?

Nothing is more effective than a review and recommendation from a raving fan. Please e-mail me your thoughts and testimonials, and please let me know whether I can include them in my next printing or on my website.

You probably have at least ten people in your professional or personal life that might benefit from this book. Please tell your friends, family, and professional associates about *Getting Your Act Together: How to Put the SHOW into Business*

For more information about workshops and book orders, visit my website: www.gettingyouracttogether.com
E-mail your comments to me at: barbturino@gettingyouracttogether.com

CPSIA information can be obtained at www.ICGtesting.com
Printed in the USA
LVOW091938150412

277709LV00001B/1/P